# First World War
## and Army of Occupation
# War Diary
## France, Belgium and Germany

46 DIVISION
Divisional Troops
232 Brigade Royal Field Artillery
1 January 1915 - 28 February 1917

WO95/2674/2

The Naval & Military Press Ltd
www.nmarchive.com
**Published in association with The National Archives**

Published by

The Naval & Military Press Ltd

Unit 10 Ridgewood Industrial Park,

Uckfield, East Sussex,

TN22 5QE England

Tel: +44 (0) 1825 749494

www.naval-military-press.com

www.nmarchive.com

*This diary has been reprinted in facsimile from the original. Any imperfections are inevitably reproduced and the quality may fall short of modern type and cartographic standards.*

# Contents

| Document type | Place/Title | Date From | Date To |
|---|---|---|---|
| Heading | WO95/2674/2 232 Brigade Royal Field Artillery | | |
| Heading | 46th Division Divl Artillery 1-3rd Nth Mid'd (Became:- 232nd Brigade R.F.A. Jan 1915-Feb 1917. To 4 Army. | | |
| Heading | North Midland Division. 3rd N.M. Bde R.F.A. Vol I. 1.1-4.3.15. | | |
| War Diary | S.S. City of Dunkirk | 25/02/1915 | 04/03/1915 |
| War Diary | Birchanger | 24/02/1915 | 27/02/1915 |
| War Diary | Birchanger | 21/02/1915 | 23/02/1915 |
| War Diary | Birchanger | 18/02/1915 | 21/02/1915 |
| War Diary | Birchanger | 11/02/1915 | 16/02/1915 |
| War Diary | Birchanger | 08/02/1915 | 11/02/1915 |
| War Diary | Birchanger | 01/01/1915 | 05/03/1915 |
| Heading | 121/4816 46 Div N.M. Division 1/3rd N.M. Bde R.F.A. Vol II 4-31.3.15 | | |
| War Diary | S.S. City of Dunkirk | 04/03/1915 | 05/03/1915 |
| War Diary | Havre | 05/03/1915 | 06/03/1915 |
| War Diary | Hazebrouck | 07/03/1915 | 07/03/1915 |
| War Diary | Ledringhem | 07/03/1915 | 10/03/1915 |
| War Diary | Fletre | 11/03/1915 | 12/03/1915 |
| War Diary | Ferme de Trois Portes near Sailly | 13/03/1915 | 13/03/1915 |
| War Diary | Near Sailly | 13/03/1915 | 15/03/1915 |
| War Diary | Near Merris | 16/03/1915 | 20/03/1915 |
| War Diary | Merris | 21/03/1915 | 21/03/1915 |
| War Diary | Armentieres | 22/03/1915 | 25/03/1915 |
| War Diary | Merris | 26/03/1915 | 30/03/1915 |
| War Diary | Near Merris | 31/03/1915 | 31/03/1915 |
| Heading | 121/5255 46th Division 3rd N.M. Bde R.F.A. Vol III | | |
| War Diary | Merris | 01/04/1915 | 01/04/1915 |
| War Diary | Kemmel | 01/04/1915 | 30/04/1915 |
| Heading | 46th Division 121/55/3 3rd N.M. Bde R.F.A. Vol IV 1-31.5.15 | | |
| War Diary | Kemmel | 01/05/1915 | 31/05/1915 |
| Heading | 46th Division 121/5971 3rd N.M. Bde R.F.A. Vol V 1-30.6.15 | | |
| War Diary | Kemmel | 01/06/1915 | 15/06/1915 |
| War Diary | Near Kemmel | 16/06/1915 | 18/06/1915 |
| War Diary | Kemmel | 19/06/1915 | 22/06/1915 |
| War Diary | Kruistraat | 23/06/1915 | 30/06/1915 |
| Heading | 46th Division 121/6243 1/3 N.M. Bde R.F.A. Vol VI 1-31-7-15. | | |
| War Diary | Kruistraat | 01/07/1915 | 17/07/1915 |
| War Diary | | 18/01/1915 | 18/01/1915 |
| War Diary | Kruistraat | 19/07/1915 | 31/07/1915 |
| Heading | 46th Division 1/3rd N.M. Bde R.F.A. Vol VII 1-26.8.15. | | |
| War Diary | Kruistraat | 01/08/1915 | 08/08/1915 |
| War Diary | Kruistraat | 01/08/1915 | 26/08/1915 |
| Heading | 46th Division 121/7121 1/3 N.M. Bde R.F.A. Vol VIII Sept 15. | | |
| War Diary | Dickebusch | 02/09/1915 | 30/09/1915 |

| | | | |
|---|---|---|---|
| Heading | 46th Division 121/7570 1/3rd N.M. Bde R.F.A. Oct 1915 Vol IX | | |
| War Diary | Vieux Berquin | 01/10/1915 | 01/10/1915 |
| War Diary | Lillers | 02/10/1915 | 06/10/1915 |
| War Diary | Labeuvriere | 07/10/1915 | 30/10/1915 |
| Heading | 46th Division 1/3rd N.M. Bde R.F.A. Nov Vol X 121/7694 | | |
| Heading | War Diary of 3rd N.M. Bde R.F.A. from 1st to 30th November 1915. | | |
| War Diary | Labeuvriere | 01/11/1915 | 04/11/1915 |
| War Diary | St. Floris | 05/11/1915 | 16/11/1915 |
| War Diary | Bout Deville | 17/11/1915 | 30/11/1915 |
| Heading | War Diary. 3rd North Midland Brigade. R.F.A. December 1st: to 31st: 1915. | | |
| War Diary | Bout Deville | 01/12/1915 | 03/12/1915 |
| War Diary | St. Venant | 04/12/1915 | 31/12/1915 |
| Heading | 1/3 N.M. Bde R.F.A. Jan 1916 Vol XII | | |
| War Diary | St. Venant | 01/01/1916 | 09/01/1916 |
| War Diary | Between St. Venant and Marseille | 10/01/1916 | 11/01/1916 |
| War Diary | Marseille | 12/01/1916 | 26/01/1916 |
| War Diary | Pont Remy | 27/01/1916 | 28/01/1916 |
| War Diary | Vauchelle Les Domart | 29/01/1916 | 31/01/1916 |
| Heading | War Diary. 3rd: North Midland Brigade. R.F.A. February 1st:- 29th: 1916 Vol XIII | | |
| War Diary | Outrebois | 13/02/1916 | 20/02/1916 |
| War Diary | Vauchelle Les Domart | 01/02/1916 | 12/02/1916 |
| War Diary | Outrebois | 21/02/1916 | 29/02/1916 |
| Heading | War Diary. 3rd: North Midland Brigade. R.F.A. March 1st: to 31st: 1916. Vol XIV | | |
| War Diary | Outrebois | 01/03/1916 | 06/03/1916 |
| War Diary | Maziers | 07/03/1916 | 08/03/1916 |
| War Diary | Mt. St. Eloy | 09/03/1916 | 31/03/1916 |
| Heading | War Diary. 3rd: North Midland Brigade. R.F.A. April 1st: to 30th: 1916. Vol XV. | | |
| War Diary | Mt. St. Eloy | 01/04/1916 | 26/04/1916 |
| War Diary | Gouy En Ternois | 27/04/1916 | 30/04/1916 |
| War Diary | Mt. St. Eloy | 17/04/1916 | 23/04/1916 |
| Heading | War Diary. 232nd: Brigade. R.F.A. Late 1/3 N.M. Bde May 1st: to 31st: 1916. Vol 16. | | |
| War Diary | Gouy En Ternois | 01/05/1916 | 08/05/1916 |
| War Diary | Warlingcourt | 09/05/1916 | 23/05/1916 |
| War Diary | | 22/05/1916 | 23/05/1916 |
| War Diary | | 06/05/1916 | 06/05/1916 |
| Heading | War Diary. Head Quarters 232nd: Brigade. R.F.A. June 1st: to June 30th: 1916. Vol 17. | | |
| War Diary | Warlincourt | 01/06/1916 | 12/06/1916 |
| War Diary | | 10/06/1916 | 10/06/1916 |
| War Diary | Warlincourt | 24/05/1916 | 31/05/1916 |
| War Diary | | 12/03/1916 | 31/03/1916 |
| War Diary | | 11/06/1916 | 16/06/1916 |
| War Diary | | 14/06/1916 | 15/06/1916 |
| War Diary | In Front of Souastre | 17/06/1916 | 30/06/1916 |
| Heading | War Diary. 232nd: Brigade. R.F.A. July 1st: to July 31st: 1916. Vol 18. | | |
| War Diary | Just in front of Souastre | 01/07/1916 | 02/07/1916 |
| War Diary | In front of Souastre | 03/07/1916 | 04/07/1916 |

| | | | |
|---|---|---|---|
| War Diary | Bienvillers. | 05/07/1916 | 11/07/1916 |
| War Diary | In front of Beaumetz | 11/07/1916 | 14/07/1916 |
| War Diary | S of Berles | 15/07/1916 | 31/07/1916 |
| Heading | War Diary. 232nd: Brigade. R.F.A. August 1st: to August 31st: 1916. Vol 19. | | |
| War Diary | La Cauchie | 31/07/1916 | 29/08/1916 |
| War Diary | Pommier | 29/08/1916 | 30/08/1916 |
| Miscellaneous | Re. organization of Divisional Artillery. Appendix-C.R.A. 772. | 28/08/1916 | 28/08/1916 |
| Heading | War Diary. 232nd: Brigade. R.F.A. September 1st: to September 30th: 1916. Vol 20. | | |
| War Diary | Pommier | 01/09/1916 | 30/09/1916 |
| Heading | War Diary. 232nd: Brigade. R.F.A. October 1st: to October 31st: 1916. Vol 21. | | |
| War Diary | Pommier | 01/10/1916 | 31/10/1916 |
| Heading | War Diary 232nd. Brigade, R.F.A. November 1916. Vol 22 | | |
| War Diary | Pommier | 01/11/1916 | 27/11/1916 |
| War Diary | La Cauchie | 28/11/1916 | 30/11/1916 |
| Heading | War Diary. 232nd. Brigade. R.F.A. December 1st: to December 31st: 1916. Vol 23. | | |
| War Diary | La Cauchie | 01/12/1916 | 03/12/1916 |
| War Diary | Grouches | 04/12/1916 | 21/12/1916 |
| War Diary | Bienvillers | 22/12/1916 | 31/12/1916 |
| Heading | War Diary 232nd: Brigade. R.F.A. January 1st: to January 31st: 1917. Vol 24. | | |
| War Diary | Bienvillers | 01/01/1917 | 28/02/1917 |

WO/95/2674/2

232 Brigade Royal Field Artillery

46TH DIVISION
DIVL ARTILLERY

1-3RD NTH MID'D (BECAME :-
232ND BRIGADE R.F.A.
JAN ~~MAR~~ 1915-FEB 1917

TO 4 ARMY

✓

nil

46 Div

A2
a.9.6

North Midland Division

121/4634

3rd N M Bde RFA.

Vol I. 1.1 — 4.8.15.

121/4634

121/4816
46 Div

N. M. Division

1/3rd N. M. Bde RFA.

Vol II 4 — 31. 3. 15

BIRCHANGER

| | | |
|---|---|---|
| 1/1/15 | Section mounted Parades | |
| 2/1/15 | The 6th Batty again carried out operations at Felsted. | |
| | The remainder of the Brigade did extending practice. | |
| 3/1/15 | Whole Holiday for Final of Stnart worthy Football Cup. 6th Batty returned from Felsted. | |
| 4/2/15 | The adjutant gave a lecture to officers on the use of the YPRES maps recently issued. | |
| 4 and 5/3/15 | The Divisional Sanitary Officer lectured the Brigade on Vaccination the | aeon |

War Diary 3rd N. Mid Bde

BIRCHANGER.

| | | |
|---|---|---|
| 8/2/15. | Vaccination began. Brigade took part in Divisional Skeleton Operations | Major H. V. de Satge proceeded to the front for 14 days instruction with a Regular Battery |
| 9/2/15 | The C/O lectured all officers on notes from the front | |
| 10/2/15 | The IOM inspected the recent extension of gun shields. | |
| 11/2/15 | Brigade Route march. The telephone cart laid out nearly 8000 yards of wire in 55 minutes moving ahead of the Brigade, communicating with the base operator | aeom |

| | | |
|---|---|---|
| Bishops Stortford 11/2/15 Contin. | War Diary 3rd N.M. Bde R.F.A. being successfully kept up while the cart was in motion from an operator seated on the cart. Conversation was quite clear | |
| 12/2/15. | Brigade Skeleton Parade. Night operations were carried out in Hallingbury Park. | |
| 15/2/15. | Laying & Fuze setting Tests. Officers carried out Pistol practise for the first time, after having been mobilized for over 6 months. | |
| 16/2/15. | Brigade skeleton Parade. | a.c.c.m. |

War Diary 1/3rd N. M. F. A Bde

BIRCHANGER

18/2/15. The GOCRA inspected the Brigade during a Route march.

Orders having been received that the Brigade must be ready to move at any moment, the afternoon parade both today and yesterday consisted of foot drill with a view to inspection by H.M. the King on Friday next.

5

19/2/15 The Division was Inspected by H.M. the King in Great Hallingbury Park.

21/2/15. Brigade Route march and Inspection. aeron

Much inconvenience is

| | | |
|---|---|---|
| 21/2/15 | caused by the fact that new harness is often supplied without regard to the type of horse for which it is required, & is consequently found to be either much too small or much too big. | |
| | Officers completed Pistol practice so far as possible, considering that the full amount of ammunition has never been supplied. | |
| 23/2/15 | The Brigade was warned for departure overseas on Saturday next. | ACOM |

War Diary 1/3rd N.M. FA Bde

Bircharges
24/2/15 The Brigade was inspected, by units, in marching order.

25-26 2/15 Completion of Equipment before proceeding abroad.

26-27 2/15 The Brigade entrained by 1/2 Batteries & 1/5th Amm Col, at Bishops Stortford for Southampton, in 6 trains, the 1st being due to start at 12.10 a.m & the last at 10.10 a.m

27/2/15 The Brigade arrived at Southampton and went into "rest Camp".

acom

War Diary 1/3rd N. Mid. F.A. Bde. 

S.S. City of Dunkirk.

| | | |
|---|---|---|
| 23/2/15 8.15 pm | The Brigade embarked between 10 a.m. and 4 p.m. on<br>S.S. City of Dunkirk<br>" Huanchaco<br>" Caledonian.<br>The arrangements at the "rest camp" were exceedingly bad, there being no shelter or permanent lines for horses, & no hutments available for the men | |
| 28-4/3/15 | S.S. City of Dunkirk with Brigade Headquarters, 1/2 5th Batty, 2/6 R.A.M.C. and 1/2 company ~~[illegible]~~ infantry, remained in dock. Men did physical drill and horses were exercised on the quay. | a com |

S.S. City of Dunkirk .. War Diary 1/3rd N.M. F.A. Bde 32

| | | |
|---|---|---|
| 4/3/15 6.25 p.m. | S.S. City of Dunkirk sailed for Havre with an escort of 2 destroyers. | |
| 5/3/15 3 a.m. | Arrived off Havre | |
| Havre | | |
| Midday | Disembarkation began | |
| 6 p.m. | Disembarkation completed. | |
| 7 p.m. | Part of Headquarters & whole of 6th Staffs Batty entrained at Gare des Marchandises | |
| 6/3/15 2 a.m. | Headquarters and 5th Staffs Battery entrained at Point 1 Gare des Marchandises. | |
| Hazebrouck | | |
| 7/3/15 2 am | HQs + 5th Staffs Batty detrained at Hazebrouck | |
| 5 a.m | The Ammunition Column detrained. | ocm |

War Diary 1/3° N. Mid. F. A. Bde 

| | | | |
|---|---|---|---|
| HAZEBROUCK | | | |
| 7/3/15 | 6.30am | HQs, 5th Battery and Ammunition Column marched from the Station towards LEDRINGHEM. No guide or map having been provided, the march had to be delayed until day break | ‖ N.B. |
| LEDRINGHEM | | | |
| | 2.15pm. | LEDRINGHEM was reached, where the 4th and 6th Batteries were already billeted. It being forbidden to pass through CASSEL (occupied by French troops) the march was via TERDIGHEM and HARDIFORT. The cross road running north west from the latter was almost impassable for 3/4 mile, and the | acon |

LEDRINGHEM

| | | |
|---|---|---|
| 7/3/15 contd | Ammunition Column had to partially reverse and enter LEDRINGHEM via the CASSEL = BERGUES main road. | |
| 8/3/15 | Day spent in cleaning up. | |
| 9pm | Orders received that the Division would move to a new area on following day | |
| 9/3/15 6.30 a.m. | The Brigade marched via RIETVELD = LOOGE HOCK = LE TEMPLE = STEENVOORDE = EECKE to CAESTRE, where the Division marched past General Sir SMITH-DORRIEN. The Brigade then proceeded to its new billeting area just South of FLETRE = METEREN | |
| 2.30pm | main road, where it was billeted in 7 farms. | acou |
| 10/3/15. 7pm | Brigade Headquarters moved to FLETRE. | |

FLETRE. WAR DIARY 1/3rd N Mid. F A Bde. 35

| | | |
|---|---|---|
| 11/3/15. 10·30am. | Orders received that the Division was to be ready to move at 11 a. m | |
| 1p m. | The Brigade moved via METEREN = BAILLEUL = LE KIRLEN = LE PETIT MORTIER to an area just N.W. of SAILLY sur LE LYS, where units were billeted in various farms. | |
| 12 p m | Orders received to be ready move at one hour's notice after 6 a. m. | |
| 12/3/15 5·30pm | Orders received from CRA that the 7th Division had broken through the German line between PIETRE and Moulin de PIETRE and were advancing in direction of Rue DENFER, and that N. Mid Division would be ready to move at any time after 6 a. m. tomorrow. | acon |

| | | |
|---|---|---|
| Ferme de TROIS PORTES near SAILLY | WAR DIARY 1/3rd N. Mid F A Bde | |
| 13/3/15. 5.30am | The C/O, adjutant, Orderly officer, BSM. Telephone Wagon, Battery Commanders, observing officers, and telephonists, met the G.O.C.R.A. at ROUGE DE BOUT one mile S.E. of SAILLY station and subsequently reconnoitred gun positions along the road running N.E. from ROUGE DE BOUT with a view to firing on FROMELLES. Observing stations were chosen on parallel roads 2000-2500 yards in front. Arrangements were made to billet with the 3rd F.A. Bde. of the Canadian Division, whose Batteries were in action against the enemy's trenches N.W. of FROMELLES | a crown |

| | | |
|---|---|---|
| 13/3/15. | and occupied positions just in front of road along which positions for this Brigade were chosen. Over a mile of wire ~~had been~~ was laid out from Headquarters towards the observing stations. | |
| 1.30pm | Orders were received that the marching orders of the Division were cancelled & the Brigade was to return to existing Billets. Positions had been to some extent prepared, but no battery had moved out from existing billets. | |
| 2.30pm | Moved back to billets. | |
| 14/3/15 | Nothing to report, except heavy firing | in direction of S^t ELOI. |
| 15/3/15 9a.m. | The Brigade marched to a new Billeting area in the neighbourhood of BLEU = MERRIS about 5 miles N.W. of existing Billets. | a corn |
| 11.30am | Reached new billets which were just being vacated by the Oxfordshire Huzzars | |

near MERRIS — War Diary 1/3rd N. Mid F A Bde. 

| | | |
|---|---|---|
| 16/3/15. 9pm. | Nothing to report. | |
| 17/3/15 to 20/3/15 | Training proceeded as usual, special attention being given to telephonists and the laying out of lines of fire by night with lanterns. On the 19th orders were received that a proportion of officers NCO's + men were to proceed on attachment to the 6th Division from the 21st Inst. On the 20th orders were received that the whole Brigade was to be attached. Later on the 20th orders were received that only 1 Battery + a proportion of Headquarters were to be attached. | a corr |

MERRIS

| Place / Date / Hour | Summary of Events | Remarks |
|---|---|---|
| 21/3/15 8.a.m | The c/o orderly officer BSM & 2 telephonists proceeded to ARMENTIERES on a tour of Instruction, reaching there about 1pm at (6th Division) 38th Bde HQrs | |
| ARMENTIERES 7.p.m | The 4th Battery arrived from MERRIS for instruction and took up a position 1½ miles from ARMENTIERES on the LA VESEÉ road, and built emplacements screened by brushwood | |
| 22/3/15. | The 4th Batty registered 2 houses at WEZ MACQUART (A & B in appendix A) firing 40 rounds. Shooting was accurate | acw |

ARMENTIERES.

| | | |
|---|---|---|
| 23/3/15. | 40 rounds were again fired during the day.<br><br>The G.O.C. Division (General Keir) and the G.O.C.R.A. Division (Gen. Paget) visited the Battery.<br><br>The targets registered were as shewn in appendix A. | appendix A. |
| 24/3/15. | 40 rounds fired.<br><br>Shooting good at over 5,500. Targets as in appendix A. | |

| | | |
|---|---|---|
| ARMENTIERES 25/3/15. | 40 rounds again fired. Targets were as in in Appendix A After dark the Battery came out of action and returned to Billets near MERRIS. The Headquarters party also returned. | |
| MERRIS 26/3/15. | The 5th Staffs Battery were attached to the 12th Brigade near GRIS POT for instruction | |
| 27 to 30/3/15. | Training of remaining unit continued on usual lines. | |
| 30/3/15. | The Brigade attended Church Parade at OUTTERSTEEN, where the Bishop of LONDON preached | ACEM |

WAR DIARY 1/3rd N Mid F A Bde 42 ~~99~~

| | | |
|---|---|---|
| near MERVIS. 31/3/15 | The 5th Batty returned from attachment. Firing was as shewn in Appendix B. Orders received that no further attachments were to take place. | Appendix B |
| | | [illegible] |

[signature]
Lieut Col.
Commdg 1/3rd N Mid F A Bde

121/5255

46th Division

3rd N.M. Bde RFA.

Vol III

MERRIS War Diary 3rd N. Mid. Bde R F A

| | |
|---|---|
| 1/4/15 | |
| 7.30 am | Headquarters and unit Commanders proceeded to HQ 5th Div. RA near LOCRE and thence to mount KEMMEL to see positions. |
| KEMMEL 8 pm | Batteries took up positions just N.W. of Mt KEMMEL. Brigade HQs established at the CHALET in KEMMEL. Observing stations occupied on Mt KEMMEL. Ammunition Column at CROIX de POPERINGHE. Gun positions are those of the 28th Bde who are moving elsewhere. |
| | The Brigade is attached to 5th Divl. R.A. and for night firing is under O/C RHA Bde consisting of G.H.&J. Batteries (Col. Rotton) |

[illegible]

War diary 3rd N. M. Bde R.F.A.

KEMMEL

| | | |
|---|---|---|
| 2/4/15 | Batteries registered German trenches from S. edge of PETIT BOIS to VAN DEN BERGHE farm, covering our trenches K1 K2 J3 | Ref. map 28 S.W. 1/20,000 |
| 3/4/15 | Registration continued. | |
| 4/4/15 | A forward observing officer was detailed to observe for the Brigade in trench K1 | |
| 5/4/15 | 1st Derbyshire Howitzer Battery was attached to the Brigade | |
| | The 4th Battery moved one section to a new position about 1 mile N. of KEMMEL | N 15 6 8.4 on Ref. map. |
| 6/4/15 | Remainder of 4th Battery moved into the new position. Owing to breaking of telephone line communication could not be had with forward observing officer. The 5th Battery | |

War diary 3rd N. M. Bde R F A

KEMMEL

| | | |
|---|---|---|
| 6/4/15 (contin). | and Ammunition Column reconnoitred new positions | |
| 7/4/15 | Brigade zone altered to cover trenches H4, J1 and J2 + J3 (North edge of PETIT BOIS to S. corner of WHYTSCHAETE wood) 4th and 6th Batteries registered on H4 and J3 | |
| 8/4/15. | Positions of units now are as follows:- | Ref map 28 S.W. 1/20000 |
| | Headquarters N 21 c 8 6 | |
| | 4th Battery N 15 b 8 4 | |
| | 5th Battery N 15 d 5 5 | |
| | 6th Battery N 24 c 9 5 | |
| | Amm. Col. Mont NOIR (M 21 c 1 8.) | |
| | 1st Devon Battery N 15 b 2 8. | |
| | A slightly different zone | |

ccm

War diary 3 N. M. Bde. R.F.A.

| | |
|---|---|
| KEMMEL 8/4/15 (contin) | was allotted to the Brigade The zone now is as follows:– |
| | Right to left. |
| | 4th Battery MAEDELSTEDE farm to S.W. corner of WHYTSCHAETE wood. |
| | 5th Battery S.W. corner W. wood to S Corner of PETIT BOIS |
| | 6th Battery S corner of P.B. to middle of P.B |
| | During the afternoon about 30 German shell fell in neighbourhood of 4th Battery |
| 9/4/15. | Batteries registered new zones. |
| 4.60 pm. | In response to message from Notts & Derby Brigade, 6th Battery replied to enemy's HE shells falling at H4 trench |

War diary 3rd W. M. Bde. R.F.A.

| | | |
|---|---|---|
| KEMMEL 9/4/15 (contin.) | The C.R.A. N. Midland Division took over from the 5th Div. R.A. | |
| | A section of the 4th Brigade Ammunition Column were attached to this Brigade Ammunition Column | |
| 10. 4. 15. | Telephone line laid from trench H3 to Headquarters. Section of 4th Bde. Ammn. Col. left the Brigade. | |
| 11. 4. 15. | Telephone communication with forward observing officers established.<br>Three RA officers attached to Batteries to instruct, as follows:—<br>Capt Lucas — 5th Batty.<br>Sir John Keen — 6th<br>Major Ward — 4th | |
| | Registration was interrupted | a c o m |

KEMMEL War Diary 3rd N Mid Bde RFA

| | |
|---|---|
| 11.4.15 (contin.) | by appearance of a captive airship over WHYTSCHAETE from about 1.30 till 5.30 |
| | 6th Battery registered on trenches in front of PETIT BOIS. 5th & 4th Batteries registered trench H3 |
| 12./4/15 | During the night 5th Batty fired 2 rounds and 6th four rounds in response to call from infantry |
| 10 am. | Enemy dropped 6" shells on DICKEBOSCH LA CLYTTE road. |
| 10.25 am | Captive airship again seen near WHYTSCHAETE. |
| 2.50 pm | Enemy dropped 2 6" inch shells 300 yds to left flank of 4th Battery. |
| 3.35 pm | Enemy began shelling trench H3, switching later to H2 & then to H1. All Batteries replied. |

aeum

KEMMEL 12.4.15. War Diary 3rd N M Bde RFA

| | |
|---|---|
| 5.35 pm | Enemy ceased shelling, but began again at 5.55 pm |
| | Major B.J.T. Ford was taken to a rest hospital at ST JANS CAPPEL. |
| | The system now is for a subaltern to sleep each night at HQs of 6th Battalion Notts & Derby Brigade & proceed to H3 trench before dawn remaining there till dusk. |
| 13/4/15. | Zeppelin passed over during the night & dropped several bombs in LOCRE. |
| 3.30 pm | Enemy shelled H3, just after 5th Battery had stopped registering. All Batteries replied and enemy ceased shelling at 4.30. |
| | Capt. F.R. Meynell took over command of 4th Battery. Sir John Keen left the 6th Batty to rejoin his own Battery. |

acorn

War Diary 3rd W. L. Bde R F A

KEMMEL

| | | |
|---|---|---|
| 14. 4. 15. | No firing by Batteries, in order to save our working parties from any chance of retaliation.<br><br>Between 4 and 6 pm 60 or more "crumps" fell in front of 4th + 5th Battery positions coming from direction of WHYTSCHAETE.<br>About 7 pm. 3 salvos of shrapnel fell near 6th Battery observing station on Little KEMMEL, probably intended for KEMMEL-LOCRE road.<br>In the early morning while carrying out a reconnaissance with the Adjutant the C/O was just missed by a sniper who apparently frequents farm buildings E of KEMMEL on E side of VIERSTRAAT road. | |

[signature]

82

War Diary 3rd Mid Bde RFA

KEMMEL.

| | |
|---|---|
| 15.4.15. | Heavy firing heard during night in direction of St Eloi |
| 12 noon. | F.O.O. reported that the enemy had planted blue & white flags on their parapet. |
| 5-6 pm. | 5th Batty registered K1 (9 rounds) + H3 one round. |
| | 4th Batty registered J3 (14 rounds). |
| | Warning received that enemy might attack at night in order to cover an attack on YPRES. |
| ~~[illegible]~~ 10.7 pm | Orders received ~~[illegible]~~ that wagon teams were to be harnessed up and men to keep their boots on, + particular alertness to be observed |
| | ~~[illegible]~~ Frequent ~~[illegible]~~ Special instructions |

aeon

KEMMEL

as to "alertness" ~~[illegible]~~ lead to ~~[illegible]~~ a tendency to slackness whenever no such orders are received. A definite order as to harnessing up etc. is of course on a different footing.

16/4/15.

4 pm. All three batteries and also the 1st Derbyshire Howitzer Batty fired a salvo on PETIT BOIS by arrangement with the infantry, in the hope of stopping snipers who enfilade our trenches from trees.

4.25 pm Two salvos enemy's shrapnel fell N20 C55 & N20 C 5.8 Four 6 inch Howitzer shells fell NE slopes of Mount KEMMEL

ACON

KEMMEL

| | | |
|---|---|---|
| 17. 4. 15. | Batteries registered on PETIT BOIS. Brigade zone changed so as to run from S.W. Corner of PETIT BOIS almost to PECKHAM FARM. | |
| 7.45 pm. | Batteries fired one salvo each on PETIT BOIS + then went to slow section fire, searching the wood. This was to prevent any counter=attack in view of our attack on Hill 60. Firing continued for 15 minutes. Germans made practically no reply. | |
| 18. 4. 15. | Report from 3rd Division that shooting of this Brigade had been very accurate. | |
| | The 6th Battery surrounded | ACDM |

KEMMEL

| | | |
|---|---|---|
| | a farm from near which a native had been seen to send off a pigeon. | Map reference for farm is N.20.A.53 |
| | Heavy firing from British guns observed in direction of St Eloi. | |
| 19.4.15. | The A.P.M. discharged the two men who had been arrested in connection with the pigeon being let go, and directed the farm to be watched. | |
| | It would seem that if civilians are sufficiently doubtful characters to be watched, they should be sent back out of the area entirely. | |
| 12.40pm | 4 gun flashes observed at true bearing 75 degrees from N26 B17. | |
| 4-5pm | 5th & 6th Batteries registered on PECKHAM. | ACM |

War Diary
3 W L Bde RFA

KEMMEL

| | | |
|---|---|---|
| 20/4/15. | During the night and morning lines were completed from trenches H4, H3 & H2 to 6th, 5th and 4th Batteries, and tests were carried with 5th & 4th Batteries, a single gun being fired in each case at call from the infantry:- 5th Battery shell arriving at German trenches in 30 sec. In the afternoon the 4th and 6th Batteries registered PECKHAM | |
| 21/4/15 | Trenches heavily shelled intermittently all day. | |
| 11-45 am | At Infantry call 6th & 5th Batteries registered on H4, & on H2 & 3 respectively | |
| 3.50 pm | 6th Batty registered on PECKHAM | |
| 22/4/15. | Trenches heavily shelled during morning. Our Batteries replied with 20 rounds altogether | A.C.M. |

| | | |
|---|---|---|
| KEMMEL | | |
| 22.4.15 | | |
| Contd. | | |
| 5.45 pm | Balloon observed to descend on line drawn from N26B46 to Church at O36B36 | |
| 23.4.15 | Heavy firing heard north of YPRES, where the Germans have broken through between French & Canadians. There is a scare about poisonous gases sent into our trenches. Day passed very quietly in this area. Batteries did not fire. Lamp signalling to all batteries successfully established from close to Brigade observing position on Mount KEMMEL. | |
| 24.4.15. | During the morning Batteries fired on German trenches in answer to heavy rifle fire on an aeroplane observing for the Heavies. | aEOM |

KEMMEL

24.4.15

Tests of telephone from the trenches resulted as follows:–
Time from order given in trenches to burst of shell:–

| | |
|---|---|
| 4th Batty. | 30 secs. |
| 5th " | 25 " |
| 6th " | 35 " |

In the afternoon each battery carefully registered its own zone. Our trenches will heavily bombarded, & expect an attack any minute. Trenches much damaged by heavy trench mortars.

25.4.15

In the morning each Battery fired one gun as a test, on call from the trenches, and later registered usual zones with 9 rounds each.

At 2.20 and 3.50 pm 6th Battery fired 4 & 2 rounds respectively to stop a trench mortar, which they did.

acom

| | |
|---|---|
| KEMMEL 25.4.15 (contd.) | 2nd Lieut Thornewill + 3 other ranks joined the Brigade from Reserve unit. |
| 26.4.15. | In the afternoon the 6th Battery fired 3 rounds in reply to a Trench mortar in PETIT BOIS, which ceased firing. Afternoon passed very quietly in Brigade zone. |
| 27.4.15. | Day very quiet on this zone. |
| 5.30 pm | 4th Batty fired 6 rounds on machine gun near PETIT BOIS and also replied to some shelling of our trenches. Flashes seen 115 mag. from N20 D46 |

ACWM

KEMMEL

| | |
|---|---|
| 27/4/15 contin. | Major Ford returned from Hospital to the Amm Col :- Capt Wrottesley going to 5th Batt & Capt Lee to 6th Batt. |
| 6 pm | 6th Battery fired 3 rounds on trench mortar flash in PETIT BOIS. Too misty to observe. |
| 28.4.15 | Between 9 & 11 am. trenches were heavily shelled with HE's and trench mortar. 5th & 6th Batteries replied. Afternoon passed very quietly. Very heavy firing north of YPRES. |
| 29.4.15. 10.30 to 3 pm | Trenches were heavily shelled. Batteries replied, firing 37 rounds in all. The heavies ought to be in much closer communication with the trenches. They cannot be turned on quickly enough. |

ACM

War Diary 3rd N. M. Bde R F A

KEMMEL

| | | |
|---|---|---|
| 29. 4. 15. 10.20 pm. | Zeppelin reported to be coming over from trenches. | |
| 30. 4. 15. | Batteries registered over usual zones. Two new trench mortars were fired on enemy's redoubt near SPANBRUCKMOLEN | |
| | | ac/lm |

C. J. Gowa Lt Col.
Comdg 3rd N M Bde R F A.

46th Division

121/55/3

3rd N.M. Bde RFA.

Vol IV 1 — 31.5.15

KEMMEL
1.5.15

Between 4 and 6 pm enemy's shrapnel fell on eastern slopes of Mt KEMMEL.

6.15 pm 5th Battery fired 3 rounds over H4 trench in reply to enemy's shelling and 2 rounds on Trench mortar in PETIT BOIS which ceased fire.

5th Battery fired further 8 rounds over H3 in reply to shelling of trenches

over

KEMMEL

| | | |
|---|---|---|
| 1.5.15. | | |
| 8.25pm | 6" Battery fired salvo on enemy's mortars in PETIT BOIS which ceased fire. | |
| 2.5.15. | | |
| 1.45pm | 6" Battery fired 3 rounds on enemy's working party in PETIT BOIS. On the whole this zone very quiet. | |
| 3.5.15. | 6.55 am 6" Battery fired on working party in PETIT BOIS | |
| 5.45pm | 6" Battery in conjunction with 1st Derbyshire Battery fired 8 rounds on what is supposed to be the | Ochm |

| | | |
|---|---|---|
| KEMMEL | head of a shaft in PETIT BOIS. There has been a good deal of trench work done during the last few days by the enemy. Possibly arrangements are being made to install asphyxiating gas cylinders | |
| 3.30pm. | 4th & 5th Batteries replied to heavy rifle fire and shelling, over H2, & 3, and G4 | |
| 7pm | Our 2 new trench mortars fired on SPANBROEKMOLEN, and successfully drew HE retaliation onto a dummy emplacement by firing rifles charged with black powder. | [illegible] |

War Diary 3rd N. Mid Bde RFA

| | | |
|---|---|---|
| KEMMEL | | |
| 4. 5. 15. | | |
| 4pm. | 6th Battery fired on enemy's increasing earthwork at South side of PETIT BOIS. | |
| 5. 5. 15. | | |
| 6.30pm. | Heavy shelling of our trenches by Trench mortars along edge of PETIT BOIS and WHYTSCHAETE wood. 5th & 6th Batteries replied with 4 and 29 rounds respectively. | |
| | Training of signallers in use of Heliograph proceeding. | |
| 6.5.15. | Nothing to report. Major Ford invalided home. | |
| 7.5.15. | All Batteries registered PETIT BOIS. 6th & 5th Batteries retaliated with 3 + 4 rounds respectively on enemy's shelling of our trenches | |
| | | ACOM |

War Diary 3' N. Mid Bde RFA

| | | |
|---|---|---|
| KEMMEL | | |
| 8. 5. 15. | Nothing to report | |
| | Capt. Lee took over Command of Amm - Col | |
| 9. 5. 15. | | |
| 11am. | 5' Batty registered usual zone with 12 rounds. | |
| 7pm | on explosion of our mine at PECKHAM all batteries opened fire in case of developments. 44 rounds expended | |
| 10. 5, 15. | | |
| 9.30am | 6' Batty fired 2 rounds on PETIT BOIS working party. and again 3 rounds at | |
| 5pm. | 5pm 4' Batty fired 4 rounds in answer to heavy rifle fire at PECKHAM | [illegible] |

War Diary 3rd N Mid Bde R F A

KEMMEL

| | |
|---|---|
| 11. 5. 15. | |
| 2.30pm. | All Batteries fired salvos in succession at pre-arranged targets in conjunction with aeroplane observation. No corrections were given; the observer merely firing a red light for Batteries to be ready and a green light for fire. |
| 8.46pm | 6' Batty fired salvo on PETIT BOIS in reply to French mortar |
| 12. 5. 15 | |
| 3.30pm. | 6' Battery fired 10 rounds on working party in PETIT BOIS. |
| 7.45pm. | Enemy shelled the garden of KEMMEL Chateau with small H.E. |

A Cotton

KEMMEL

13.5.15.

| | |
|---|---|
| 6.40pm | 4th Battery fired 4 rounds over H2 trench in retaliation on on enemy's shelling, which ceased. |
| 6.50pm | 6th Battery fire 6 rounds on WAYTSCHAETE WOOD in reply to enemy's shelling near KEMMEL |
| 7.15pm | All batteries went to slow Battery fire in answer to heavy shelling of our trenches, which ceased. |
| 14.5.15. | In the morning enemy registered 4th Battery position with 3 rounds shrapnel. |
| 12.50pm | 5 & 6th Batteries replied to shelling of H3. Enemy's guns switched. |

Ocom

| | | |
|---|---|---|
| K[illegible]ME4 | | |
| 14.5.15 (Contd) | | |
| 1.25 pm | 4th Battery registered usual zones with 16 rounds. | |
| | Reconnaissance made of possible positions for advancing a single gun from each battery beyond the 2nd line of trenches to cover a retirement. | |
| | The proposal would have the effect of making a comparatively slow firing gun attempt the work of machine guns, with a grave risk of losing 25% of guns. The difficulties of ammunition supply would also be very great, while the ~~effect~~ advantages would not appear to be any greater than if the gun remained in its battery with no risk of being lost. | ACM |

| | |
|---|---|
| KEMMEL 15.5.15 (continued) | Between 12 noon & 2 pm there was heavy shelling of our trenches. All Batteries replied |
| 3.45 pm | 6th Battery registered a house in WHYTSCHAETE with a green shutter, suspected to be a place of observation. In the morning the enemy again registered 4th Battery gun position |
| 16.5.15. | In the afternoon the 5th Battery billets were shelled and two men wounded |
| 17.5.15. | Day very quiet. |
| 4 pm. | 6th Battery silenced machine gun in enemies' trenches |

Acorn

KEMMEL

| | |
|---|---|
| 17.5.15. (contd) | ...n of wire to H3 was completed to a distance of between 4 & 5 hundred yards from the trench by a party of 60 men. |
| 18.5.15. | Thick weather prevented any observation. Day very quiet. |
| 19.5.15. | Weather again very bad. Nothing to report |
| 20.5.15. | Day quiet in Brigade zone except for shelling of communication trench, and presence of hostile aeroplane which dropped lights in this Brigade area. Batteries registered German trenches and points beyond them OCom |

War Diary 3rd N Mid Bde R F A

| | |
|---|---|
| KEMMEL. 20.5.15. contin | The R H A fired a number of incendiary shell, which gave no results. |
| 21.5.15. | Nothing to report |
| 22.5.15. | Batteries registered on points behind German trenches. |
| 6.10 pm | 6th Battery fired 3 rounds in retaliation on trench mortar, and 4 |
| 6.30 pm | rounds in retaliation on shelling of our trenches which ceased. |
| 23.5.15 | Day quiet. 6th Battery registered on the Hospice WYTSCHAETE. |

Blom

KEMMEL

24.5.15.

12 noon — 6th Battery fired on extensive working party in WYTSCHAETE wood.

3.40pm — 4th Battery silenced sniping in PECKHAM

5th & 6th Batteries registered on points behind German fire trenches.

25.5.15. — Enemy have done an immense amount of work during last few days, apparently making large emplacements both behind and in front of their lines.

Incendiary shell reported to have been used by enemy on farm near KEMMEL

[illegible]

KEMMEL

| | | | |
|---|---|---|---|
| | | From a later report the cause of the fire appeared to be shrapnel | |
| 26.5.15. | | | |
| | 10.45am | Enemy reported shelled close to 4th Battery position. | |
| | | This position has now been thoroughly registered by the enemy, and in the event of heavy fighting they could put it out of action at once. | |
| | 1.15pm | 4 shrapnel fell on top of Mt KEMMEL | |
| | 5pm | Hostile aeroplane flew over 6th + 4th positions, + dropped coloured lights while returning to enemy's lines | aeron |

War Diary 3rd N. Mid. Bde R.F.A

KEMMEL

| | | |
|---|---|---|
| 27.5.15 | | |
| 5 pm. | 4th Battery fired on PECKHAM at call of Infantry to keep down Snipers. | |
| 6.20 pm. | 6th Battery fired on ~~[illegible]~~ working party. | |
| 28.5.15. | Considerable party of enemy seen wandering in WYTSCHAETE wood both morning & evening, and were fired on by 6th Battery at 4.30 pm. | |
| 29.5.15. | Apparently owing to the presence of a mounted party on the KEMMEL–LOCRE road a 6 or 8 inch HE shell fell about 50 yards from this Brigade Headquarters killing 3 small children, but doing no other damage. Road sentries are placed in a difficult position, | [illegible] |

| | | |
|---|---|---|
| KEMMEL | | |
| 29.5.15 (continued) | owing to the fact that Staff officers when asked to dismount at exposed points are apt either to ignore the sentry or expostulate with them | |
| 30.5.15. | Nothing to report. | |
| 31.5.15. | In the evening gas was reported to be distinctly detectable on M<sup>t</sup> KEMMEL and faintly in the trenches | |
| 8.30pm | 5<sup>t</sup> Battery reported Zeppelin passing westward over POPERINGHE | acom |

Ch. Gower Lt Col
Comdg 3rd N M Bde RFA
46th Div

46th Division

121/5971

3rd N.M. Bde R.F.A.

Vol V 1 — 30.6.15.

a2

a/6

War Diary 3rd N. M. Bde R.F.A.

| | |
|---|---|
| KEMMEL. | |
| 1. 6. 15. | On departure of C Battery R.H.A. 4th Staffs Battery took over their gun position. |
| | Issue of anti-gas respirators completed in Batteries. |
| 2. 6. 15. | 4th Batty registered on new zone (F5 to G4) from new position. |
| 3. 6. 15. | 5th Battery moved ~~[illegible]~~ into position of K Battery R.H.A. |
| | Zones now are:<br>4th Batty F5 to G4 } Lincs + Leicester Bde<br>5th " ~~G4~~ H2 }<br>6th " H2 to J3 } Notts + Derby Bde. |

War Diary 3rd N. M. Bde
RFA

| | | |
|---|---|---|
| KEMMEL | | |
| 4.6.15. | Between 12 noon & 12.45 enemy dropped 4 or 5 shell (apparently 8 inch) into KEMMEL killing a Col & wounding a Col of the Lincs & Leicester Bde. | |
| | The 49th Howitzer Bde from ~~Kitchener's~~ new army have taken up positions W. of Mt KEMMEL | |
| 5.6.15.<br>6.6.15 | Nothing to report. | |
| 7.6.15. | Orders received that Brigade sentries are not to ask any officers to dismount when proceeding over exposed ground near guns or wagon lines. | |
| 10.6.15. | Information received that 2 officers from the Brigade | |

KEMMEL

and 2 N.C.O's ——— may proceed on leave for 5 days at a time, on producing sufficiently urgent reasons.

A proportion per Battery and ammunition Column would be quicker, fairer, and equally convenient.

11.6.15. The Adjutant & Major de Salis proceeded on 5 days leave to England

5 crumps fell along a line from KEMMEL cross roads to little KEMMEL, 3 falling close to Brigade Headquarters.

12.6.15. Orders received from CRA to move HQrs further back.

5th & 6th Batteries fired on German working parties.

KEMMEL

| | |
|---|---|
| 13.6.15 | Brigade Headquarters moved to farm at N19c92 about 1 mile W of KEMMEL on LOCRE Road. |
| | Trenches were heavily crumped between 4 30 & 6 30 pm |
| | 4th Battery retaliated. |
| | Headquarters closed and reopened at new billet at 10 pm. |
| 14.6.15. | Frequent shelling of our trenches during the day. also bombing of mortars |
| | 5th & 6th Batteries retaliated. |
| 15.6.15. 10 am | A Communication practice was carried out. Divisional & Div R.A. Headquarters |

KEMMEL

moved forward to DRANOUTRE

Brigadiers of 130th & 139th Brigades occupied dug outs at LINDENHOEK and Siege farm on KEMMEL VIERSTRAAT road respectively.

The O/c Brigade was in Brigade observing station on Mt KEMMEL & the orderly officer with the O/c 130th Brigade. Telephonic communication was successful.

Frequent crumping of our trenches during the day. Batteries retaliated.

9 pm Very heavy rifle firing and trench mortaring in Brigade zone. J3 reported to be blown up and H3 evacuated. Batteries fired 57 rounds. Situation quiet about 9.30 pm

near KEMMEL

| | |
|---|---|
| | Major de Satge & the Adjutant returned from leave. |
| 16/6/15 | The C/O went on leave. |
| 3.30 to 4.30 am | Unusual amount of rifle fire. 4th Batty fired 8 rounds. |
| 17/6/15. | Some shelling of trenches to which 6th Battery replied |
| 18/6/15. | Orders received that the Brigade would move by halves on the 20th & 21st to positions further north. |
| 1.10 am | 4th & 5th Batteries fired salvos owing to heavy rifle fire accompanied by red lights. During the afternoon 4th & 5th Batteries fired in retaliation |

| | |
|---|---|
| HERMEL. | |
| | for enemies shrapnel, at a working party, and in support of a mine exploded at PECKHAM. |
| 19.6.15. | Officers of the Northumbrian Artillery were shown round Batteries & OP's with a view to taking over. |
| | Batteries fired at working parties, & at cross roads where movement was suspected. |
| 20.6.15. | One section per Battery moved out at 9 pm. and marched with SAA Section of Ammunition Column |

HEMMEL [illegible]

to wagon lines 1½ west of KRUISTRAAT, having been relieved by sections of the 2nd Northumbrian Brigade.

21.6.15. Remaining sections and gun sections of Column moved out at 9pm. and marched to wagon lines mentioned above.

Advanced sections relieved sections of 3rd Northumbrian Brigade in positions E of KRUISTRAAT.

22.6.15. Brigade Headquarters moved at 8.10 am. to KRUISTRAAT to take over from 3rd Northumbrian Brigade.

10pm. After an attack by the 3rd Division had ceased, the

| | |
|---|---|
| KRUISSTRAAT. | remaining sections moved into gun positions. |
| | 1st Derbyshire Battery (2nd N. M. Bde) came into action, under O/c 3rd N. M. Bde. one man wounded in 6th Batty. |
| 23.6.15. | 1 section of 1st Derbyshire Battery came into action, completing group of 4 1/2 Batteries under O/c 3rd Bde. |
| | Brigade zone as follows:- |
| | 4th Batty Trenches 1 to 5 |
| | 5th " 6 to 8 |
| | 6 " 9 to 12. |
| 24.6.15. | Batteries registered on German trenches. |
| 25.6.15 | During absence of C.R.A. on 5 days leave the O/c Brigade |

KRUISTRAAT

became acting C. R. A.

26. 6. 15. Nothing to report.

27. 6. 15. All Batteries registered on enemy's trenches.

During the night 139th Bde Headquarters were shelled and ignited.

28. 6. 15. Officers from 1st + 2nd N. Mid. Bdes came on attachment to the Bde to see trenches + gun positions, with a view to taking over in the near future.

30. 6. 15. A second attachment of officers for 2 days began.

C. H. Gower Lt. Col.
Comdg 3 N M Bde RFA
46th Divn

46th Division

121/6243

1/3 N.M. Bde R.F.A.

Vol VI

1 - 31 - 7 - 15

KRUISSTRAAT.

1.7.15. All Batteries fired at night on roads and bivouacs behind German lines.

The system of cooperation in the Division between Infantry and Artillery requires thoroughly reorganizing. The enemy have obtained the superiority in artillery fire by retaliating on our trenches with much heavier fire whenever a Battery attempts to ~~fire~~ register, with the result that while unit commanders are blamed from above for not firing enough, they are blamed by the Infantry for ~~not~~ firing at all.

KRUISTRAAT

at the same time, though retaliation by our guns (when occasionally asked for) depends for its value upon its promptness, the Infantry are strangely lax in cooperating. After 3 days in the trenches covered by this Brigade, the majority both of officers & men of the 15th Bde had no idea where the artillery wires were or how retaliation was to be asked for.

If the enemy's artillery superiority – or at any rate the impression of superiority – is to be counteracted, not only must the Infantry take a more active interest in the system of cooperation with their own artillery, but communication between Field artillery and Heavies and between the

KRUISTRAAT

| | |
|---|---|
| | Trenches and Heavies should be **direct** instead of circuitous. |
| 2.7.15. | The CRA visited the trenches covered by the Brigade with the C/O |
| 3.7.15. | Between 11.30 am and 3 pm all Batteries retaliated for shelling of trenches. |
| 4.7.15. | A piece of a 17 inch shell which fell near the YPRES Asylum about ½ mile from Brigade H.Qs, fell close to Brigade office. |
| 5.6.15. | Trenches heavily crumped during the day. 4th & 5th & 6th Batteries retaliated. |

KRUISSTRAAT

| | |
|---|---|
| 6/7/15 6.45.am. | All Batteries opened fire on enemies' trenches to mislead enemy in connection with attack further north by 6th Corps. Batteries fired 18 rds per gun. There was practically no retaliation. |
| 7&8/7/15 | Nothing to report. |
| 9.7.15 | Position of 2nd Staffs Batty was severely shelled between 5.15 p.m. & 6.15 p.m. 4th Batty fired on a strong point located in Enemys lines opposite Trench 5 at midnight – |
| 16.7.15. | 1st Staffs Batty fired on trench mortar which was bombing Trench 50 about 9.45 pm. Bombing ceased – 4th Batty again fired on |

| | | |
|---|---|---|
| KRUISSTRAAT | | |
| 10.7.15 (Cont) | Same strong point + 5th + 6th Batteries fired on roads behind enemy's lines at midnight. 5th Batty forward section was shelled at 5. p.m. | |
| 11.7.15 | Enemy shelled trenches 3 + 4 occasionally through the day + the 1st + 4th Battys retaliated. About 7. p.m. trench mortar opened on Trench ~~49~~ + 50, ~~#~~ 1st Batty retaliated + silenced trench mortar. | |
| 12.7.15. | ~~#~~ One Sect. of 2nd Lancs Batty relieved sect. of 1st Batty Staffs + came under orders of OC Bde. | |
| 13.7.15. | Hostile Batty located at J.31. A 6.2 + was shelled by 4th Batty. Remainder of 2nd Lancs Batty relieved 1st Staffs. | |
| 14.7.15 | Nothing to report. | |

| | |
|---|---|
| KRUISSTRAAT 15. 7. 15. | Batteries fired on houses & roads in rear of enemy's trenches. 2nd Lincs battery brought a gun into action at about 4000 yds range from the trenches to be used as an anti-aircraft gun. A new allotment of rear positions in the area was communicated from V Corps. also new divisional zone on the ZILLEBEKE switch line. This entails the selection & digging of new O.P.s & a new system of telephone wires. |
| 16. 7. 15 | 5th & 6th Batteries registered each others zone with the idea of changing zones under a new grouping. The system of grouping batteries for a definite task or to simplify control seems to have rather broken down under the present conditions. The four batteries in the new group are very scattered being all over 1000 yds apart. |

KROISSTRAAT

16th (cont.) — but owing to additional batteries constantly coming in, it seems difficult to avoid, unless Bde. C.O.s are completely detached from their Bdes.—
A trench mortar fired on Trenches 49 + 50 ~~at~~ 4th Batty opened fire in retaliation —

17.7.15 — 4th Batty was heavily shelled with H.E. Shrapnel for two hours about midday by a battery in in S.E. direction. Two men wounded.

18.1.15. — 5th + 6th Batteries fired over trenches 10 + 11 in retaliation.
At 6. p.m. new grouping came into force. (~~For instructions see Appendix I.~~)
The 5th battery ceared to belong to the group commanded by O.C. 3rd Bde, + the 3rd Lancs Battery came into the group which now consists of 2nd Lancs, 3rd Lancs, 4th Staffs + 6th Staffs — with the 1st Derby How.s covering the same zone but not under command of the Group Commander.

KRUISSTRAAT

19.7.15 6th Batty + 1st Derby Hows combined to shell support trenches over No 6 Trench. 2nd Lincs registered trenches 47 + 48.
Enemy dropped several shell over KRUISSTRAAT village at 8 am searching for a heavy battery. 1st Bde HQs were shelled slightly + also a point just behind 4th Batty.
3rd Div carried out a bombardment at 7 pm to the north + the Right + Left Groups of Div. Cooperated — then the Centre group did not.
Enemy retaliated by shelling KRUISSTRAAT village.
3rd Lincs fired at Trench Mortar + silenced it.

20.7.15 4th Batty withdrew their personnel from their gun position for rest in wagon line. 2nd Lincs took over their zone temporarily.

KRUISSTRAAT

| | |
|---|---|
| 21.7.15. | Nothing to report. |
| 22.7.15. | 2nd & 3rd Lancs batteries fired on working parties. 6" Batty co operated with 1st Derby Hows on an earthwork about Y 50. 2nd Lancs fired periodically throughout the night on hostile trenches opposite the point where a mine is about to be fired – |
| 23.7.15. | 2nd Lancs continued to fire as above through the day. At 7 pm the mine was fired – 2nd Lancs & 6" Staffs opened fire in support, also 1st Derbys Hows – 2nd & 3rd Lancs fired at trench mortar between 8 pm & 9 30 pm. At 9 22 pm enemy fired a mine opposite trench 50. 3rd Lancs & 6" Staffs opened fire for ¼ hour – At 2 am. 3rd Lancs opened fire opposite Trench 47 in retaliation for Trench mortar firing near Hill 60. |

KRUISSTRAAT

| | |
|---|---|
| 24.7.15 | During the evening 3rd Hwis fired several times on working parties. Just after midnight 2nd Hwis + 6th Staffs fired over Trenches 49 + 50 in retaliation to a Trench Mortar. |
| 25.7.15 | Enemy shelled ARMAGH wood + trenches 45 to 50 periodically through the day + all batteries retaliated in reply. The gun which was brought into action on the 15th inst for use against aircraft was withdrawn as it was found impracticable to use a 15 pr satisfactorily for the purpose. |
| 26.7.15 | 2nd + 3rd Hwis fired throughout the day on working parties + on hostile trenches in retaliation as called for by the infantry. 2nd Hwis co operated with Howitzer + a battery of 23rd Bde firing HE, on a machine gun emplacement opposite 49 + 50. |

K
RUISSTRAAT

| | |
|---|---|
| 27.7.15 | Batteries retaliated throughout the day on enemy's trenches. During the night 26th – 27th 4th Batty returned from rest & came into action on their old zone $A_1$ to $A_4$ – The 2nd Lancs took over the 6th Staffs zone $A_5$ to $A_7$ & the 6th Batty went out to rest – Also the 5th Batty from the left group went to rest on the 26th. During the night enemy shelled our trenches near the crater intermittently & batteries retaliated. |
| 28.7.15 | The Adjt was detailed to ~~go~~ & lecture Inf. Officers of the ~~[illegible]~~ 51st Bde 17th Div on co-operation with artillery – Batteries fired ~~[illegible]~~ periodically throughout the day at request of Infantry in retaliation to trenches being shelled – Railway Cross near 4th Staffs & KRUISSTRAAT village were shelled off & on all day. |

| | |
|---|---|
| RRV, S[illegible]MAT 28th (Contd.) | Enemy were very active with trench mortars during the night opposite 47 + A2 - Batteries were continually called on to retaliate - The Brig. 138th Bde is not satisfied with the amount of Amtn. which is fired when retaliation is called for by the infantry - Our batteries fire anything from 6 rounds up to 20 or 30, whereas the enemy often send 100 shell over on end - If amtn. is still scarce, it might be worth while not to attempt to retaliate for a few days + then really retaliate shell for shell or more - |
| 29.7.15 | A quiet day - 3rd Lincs fired over their zone three times in retaliation + also registered SW slopes of HILL 60. During night trenches 47 to 50 were heavily trench mortared + 3rd Lincs retaliated - |

| KRUISSTRAAT | |
|---|---|
| 30.7.15 3.30 am | A heavy bombardment by the enemy began, directed against trenches opposite HOOGHE + also on KRUISSTRAAT + LILLE GATE. Hostile field guns + trench mortars opened on trenches in our Zone + batteries retaliated. |
| 6am | Situation on our zone normal. |
| 9 am | 5th + 6th Batteries ordered into action from rest. |
| 12.30 pm | 4th Batty registered SW HILL 60. |
| 1.30 pm | Information received that a counter attack on trenches lost in the morning between ZOUAVE WOOD + HOOGHE would be launched at 2.45 preceded by bombardment commencing at 2 pm. Centre Group to stand by. |
| 2 pm | Bombardment commenced. |
| 2.40 – 3.40 | 2nd + 3rd Lines + 4th Staffs retaliated on German trenches in Zone + on suspected gun position in rear. |
| 3 45 pm | 138th Inf Bde reported situation on Zone normal. + 23rd Bde RGA reported our counter attack had failed – but later information |

KRUISSTRAAT

| | |
|---|---|
| 30th 7 (cont) | information showed it had been partially successful on the left. |
| 11.30 pm. | Heavy shelling commenced again. Orders received from 5th Corps that 46th Div will maintain its line at all costs. |
| 31st 7 15. 2.30 am to 4.15 am | Trenches in our zone were shelled & trench mortared. All batteries retaliated. Enemy reported to have entered N. end of ZOUAVE wood but to have been driven out by 41st Bde. |
| 5 am | 139th Bde reported situation normal on our zone. |
| 6 am ~~to 7 pm~~ to 6.40 pm | Everything remained quiet. Communications were improved to batteries & trenches. |
| 6.40 pm | Heavy bombardment started. 2nd Lincs & 4th Staffs retaliated on our zone. |
| 7 pm | Information from 23rd Bde states enemy shelling ZOUAVE wood & attack expected on the B trenches NE Sanctuary Wood. |
| 8 pm | FOO reports situation A, to A4 normal. |

| | | |
|---|---|---|
| KRUISSTRAAT 31st (cont.) 9 p.m. | 23rd Bde report B8 being attacked & SOS signal had been received from $B_4$ – 4th & 6th Staffs opened fire over $A_5$ to $A_{12}$ in support for a short time until 23rd Bde informed us that situation was well in hand & their fire was not required – FOO. reported situation $A_1$ to $A_7$ normal. | |
| 10 p.m. | Shelling in the salient diminished & musketry to NE. also began to die down. | |

C.H. Gower Lt Col.
Comdg 3 NM Bde R.F.A.

121/6695

46th Division

1/3rd N.M. Bde RFA.

Vol VII

1 – 26. 8. 15

# 3rd NM Bde RFA

RIJSSTRAAT Aug. '15 1st to 8th

Batteries remained in action in same positions South & west of ZILLEBEKE LAKE. The enemy appeared very active with working parties about ZWARTELEEN just East of Hill 60 & they were constantly fired at. It was feared that an installation of liquid fire or gas was being put in. The batteries considerably improved their communication with the trenches. By the 8th each battery had three lines, one air line, one private buried line & one other buried line which is shared with other units. The air line is now being relaid so as to pass near a point half way to the trenches. This point will have a threefold use.

(a) All wires will be tapped there & it will act as a

| | |
|---|---|
| KRUISSTRAAT Aug 1st to 8th | relay station for linesmen –<br>(b) it will be the Observing station for the B.C. in the event of our infantry falling back.<br>(c) it will be used as a transmitting station for visual signalling from trenches to battery when lines break down –<br>The linesmen permanently stationed there will have signalling flags + lamps which they will use occasionally for practise – |
| 9th Aug | The 6th Div. carried out an attack on the trenches captured by the enemy a week previous. Orders for Centre group. Appendix I.<br>At 2.45 am the batteries opened fire on their zones, the centre of which is a point in our line about 2000 yds South of the HOOGE where the 6th Div. were attacking –<br>The 6th Staff Batty was detailed as a counter battery + opened fire on a hostile battery |

| | |
|---|---|
| KRUISSTRAAT 9th Aug (cont) | previously registered by aeroplane. |
| | The programme was successfully carried out as ordered & |
| 9 am | at 9 am 6th Div reported that all trenches previously lost had been recaptured & were being consolidated. The situation on our zone remained normal except for heavy shelling behind our trenches in SANCTUARY wood. |
| 3 pm. | At 3 pm the enemy began a heavy bombardment of the captured line from all round the salient. |
| 6 pm | This continued till 6 pm & died away at dusk. The night passed quietly. Throughout the day communications held up excellently. Although several wires were broken no battery completely lost touch with the trenches at any time. |
| | Lieut P.B. Smith joined the Bde from England. |

| | | |
|---|---|---|
| RUISSTRAAT 10th to 17th | Nothing to report – | |
| 18th Aug | At 5.30 pm the Heavies bombarded salients opposite 47 + 49 – 2nd Lines put forward a gun to assist at close range with great success – Operation Order 82 | Appendix II |
| | At the hour arranged for the bombardment, the enemy attacked near HOOGE + the SOS call was received by 6th Div. batteries – The left group opened fire, + the 5th Staffs attached to them fired at a rapid rate for a short time – The attack was apparently nullified by fire of Heavies – | |
| 19th Aug. | A redistribution of front was ordered – Operation Order 3. | Appendix III |
| | The 5th Staffs remain detached in 23rd Bde Group + the 6th Staffs also join this group, the whole coming under 3rd Div – This leaves only 4th Staffs, 2nd + 3rd Lincs in the Group – | |
| | Leave opened. Lieut's J.G. + C.R. Anson go. | |

| | |
|---|---|
| RUISSTRAAT. 20th Aug. | Major Bridges Brig.-Maj. having fallen ill Capt. Stirling Adj. of this Brigade was summoned to Div. Hqrs to take his place temporarily, & Capt. Wortley became act. Adj. |
| | The |
| 21st Aug. | The command of left group passing to Col. Campbell Johnston, O.C. 1st Brigade, & batteries were being distributed as follows, 5th & 6th Batteries under 23rd Brig. group (3rd Divn) & 4th Batt. in left group, Brig. Hqrs was no longer required in the line, & was ~~to rest~~ ordered to go to rest. |
| 22nd Aug. | Bde. Hqrs went to rest at G.24, b,8,6. The forward section of the 5th Battery, which had till now occupied a position about 1000 yards E.N.E. of the rear section, i.e. on N. end of Zillebeke Lake was withdrawn & placed alongside the rear section, near Trois Rois. |
| 26th Aug. | Maj. de Gaspé & Capt Lee went on leave. (7 days from 27th) |

[illegible signature] Lt Col.

3 N M Bde RFA.

46th Division

121
7131

1/3 N.M. Bde R.F.A.

Vol XIII

Sep 15

War Diary – 3rd N.M. Bde R.F.A.
Sept: 1915

DICKEBUSCH.



| | |
|---|---|
| 2.IX.15. | Brigade Headquarters and Battery wagon lines moved to H 26 a 7.8. |
| 7.30 pm | The 4th Battery was shelled. One NCO was killed, an ammunition dump blown up. Major Coddick who behaved with great coolness in looking for some 5th Batty men & had earlier in the afternoon been of great assistance to the 5th Lancers during heavy shelling of their rest dugouts, was wounded in the hand & evacuated. |
| 3 IX.15. | Major Meynell & Capt. Wetherby went on leave, the place of the latter as a/Adjutant being taken by Lt Morgan. |
| | In the afternoon the SOS call was received by 4th Batty from Trenches 49 & 50. The enemy were successfully silenced. |

| | | |
|---|---|---|
| 5th Sept. | Lt Col. Lawson Jones went on leave. | |
| 11th Sept. | Capt. Wolseley returned from leave, & resumed duties as A/Adj. Capt Stirling & Capt Rainbird went on leave. | |
| 13th | Lt Col. Lawson Jones returned from leave. On this day a redistribution of the various group commands of the 3rd Div. Artillery came into effect, vide Operation Orders based on O.O. No 23 of 3rd Div. | Appendix IV |
| | As a result the batteries remained in the same Divisions, i.e. 4th in 46th Divn, & 5th & 6th in 3rd Div. But Lt Col. Lawson Jones with Hqrs 3rd R.M. Brig, now went up & took command of Rt group, 3rd Div, consisting of 5th & 6th Ct Batteries & 107. The zone of trenches allotted was from A7 to halfway up B.3. then occupied by the 9th Infantry Brigade. | |

| | |
|---|---|
| 12 noon. | Maj. Hamilton, commanding 23rd Brigade R.F.A. came over, & went with Hqrs to visit. |
| 14th | 107 had orders to fire 100 rounds experimental rounds of H.E. But this order was cancelled before any of the rounds were fired. |
| 15th. | A concerted shoot on Bodmin Copse was arranged between O.C. & 9th Infantry. All 3 batteries fired on the precincts of Bodmin Copse at 9.30 p.m., ceasing fire at 9.45. |
| 17th | 46th Div. on our right had bombarded from 11 a.m. to noon. The enemy retaliated on A5 to 12, whereupon 5th & 6th Staffs retaliated, firing about 80 rounds. Upon this the enemy ceased fire |
| 18th | Col. Hutchison joined. This was the 1st day of [illegible] days bombardment to be concentrated on the enemy's trenches running across S. of the Ypres road at Hooge, preparatory to an assault to be delivered on that front by the 3rd Division. From 2-2.40 p.m. 107 fired 60 rounds |

(cont^d from p. 19.

| | |
|---|---|
| 18th Sept. (cont^d) | on enemy's trenches (1st & 2nd line), a triangle Q.20, 21, & 30. (Ref. 1/5000) |
| | 5th & 6th Siege were ordered to fire on enemy's front line, A.4 – A.11, by way of diversion. |
| 18/19 . 9.15. | During the night a redistribution of the Infantry took place, 9th Inf. Bde extending to their left, & relieving 8th Bde, who went into Corps Reserve. The 9th now took over C.1. & its main & subsidiary trenches, in addition to their existing front – A 4 – B.8. |
| | In the corresponding regrouping of Artillery 108 & 109 were added to the Right Group, which therefore now included all 3 batteries of 23rd Bde. & 5th & 6th Siege, & covered the zone A.4 – B.8. |
| Midnight. | Reliefs were completed at midnight, & the regrouping of D.A. took place at the same time. |
| 19/9/15. 9.50 a.m. | Second days programme of bombardment:– started at 9.50 a.m. 107 fired on C.T.'s, 108 & 109 on line just S. of Menin Rd. |
| | Enemy retaliated on Sanctuary Wood and B.3 in afternoon, whereupon 107, 108, 109, 5th & 6th |
| 5 – 6.30 p.m. | Sieges all turned on to wood in rear of enemy's line. |
| | H.Qrs now moved across the road to H.Qrs vacated by 9th Inf. Brigade, who went forward to Zillebeke Lake. |
| | Capt. Stirling returned from leave. |
| | The spare trench C.1, was allotted to 109. |

| | |
|---|---|
| 19/9/15. | Capt Holt & Lt. [illegible] Smith went on leave. |
| 20/9/15. 4.5 p.m. | <u>3rd Days programme of bombardment</u> started at 4.5. p.m. But 107 was only able to fire a few rounds, as Enemy balloon went up in a position which enabled it to locate flashes. 108 + 109 again took on wire. |
| 21/9/15 | <u>4th Days programme of bombardment</u> started at 5.5 a.m. 107 were again stopped owing to balloon – & this fact was reported immediately to Hqrs. D.A. |
| | On this day the command of Right group was taken over by Col. de la [illegible] & Hqrs 23rd Brigade & Hqrs. 3rd Brigade again returned to rest. |
| 2 p.m. | Handed over at 2 p.m. |
| 22nd to 24th | Bombardments carried out daily. ~~[illegible]~~ |
| 25th | Attack on HOOGE by 3rd & 14th Div on both sides of the MENIN road & against BELLEWARDE farm. 5th & 6th Batteries covered the right flank of the attack. During the day 5th Bty fired over 1000 rounds & at one time succeeded in maintaining a rate of Bty fire, one second for several minutes. |

DICKEBUSCH

| | |
|---|---|
| 26th Sept. 15 | Lieut Blackhead joined the Bde from England. |
| 27th Sept. | Lieut Viscount Sandon was seriously wounded in Trench A8 machine gun emplacement about 12.30 pm. He was about to observe fire when he was shot through both cheeks the bullet passing through his tongue. Capt Gill & Lieut W E Pearman Smith returned from leave & Lieuts Morgan & J G Anson proceeded on leave. Lieut J H Thursfield produced first performance of the Divisional Entertainment known as the "Whizbangs". |
| 28th Sept. | Orders received that Bde HQrs would shortly go up from rest & take over command of the three batteries again. Subsequently information was received that the whole Division would shortly move to a new area. |

DICKEBUSCH

| | |
|---|---|
| 29th Sept. | One Section of each battery was withdrawn from action & relieved by sections of 42nd Bde 3rd Div. – Officers were recalled from leave. |
| 30th Sept. | Remaining sections were withdrawn & Bde concentrated in wagon lines – 4th Bty position was heavily shelled during the afternoon. Lieut. Haslam & Warner were posted to the Bde temporarily from D.A.C. Orders were received that Bde would proceed to XI Corps area by march on following day |

Gower Lt Col.
Comdg. 3 N M Bde
R.F.A.

46th Division

121/7570

Z

1/3rd N.M. Bde R.F.A.

Oct 1915

Vol IX

# 3rd N. M. Bde R.H.A.

| | |
|---|---|
| VIEUX BERQUIN 1st October 1915 | The Bde marched from DICKEBUSCH at 5.30 pm + reached its new billets one mile South of VIEUX BERQUIN at 11.pm |
| LILLERS 2nd Oct. | Marched at 6.30 pm + arrived at new billets 2½ miles north of LILLERS at 12 midnight. |
| 3rd 4th 5th | Nothing to report. |
| 6th Oct. | Marched at 11 am to LABEUVRIERE + billeted there. |
| LABEUVRIERE 7th to 12th Oct | The Brigade remained in rest + went on with training. Parties of officers went up daily to study the ground between the HOHENZOLLERN REDOUBT and LOOS. On the 10th Maj. Gen Haking Cmdg XI Corps addressed the officers of the division + explained the task allotted to the XI Corps which consists of Guards Divn 12th Divn + 46th Divn. The task for 46th Divn was to taken the HOHENZOLLERN redoubt + FOSSE No 8. |

| | | |
|---|---|---|
| LABEUVRIÈRE Oct. 12th (cont.) | Orders were received that the attack would take place on the 13th. Only one battery of the 1st Bde & the 4th How Bde of the Div! Artillery were to be employed in the attack. Each Bde found one officer & 10 men to man a Smoke Bomb Mortar. Lieut A.C.O. Morgan was detailed for this duty & 10 men from Amtn. Col. They proceeded to join the 138th Inf Bde, their duty being to form a screen of smoke to cover the infantry while consolidating a captured trench. | |
| Oct. 13th. | In addition to the "smoke bomb" party the Amm. Col found a fatigue party of 8 men & 5 N.C.O.'s who were under the command of Lt Thursfield. From the statements of the survivors of Lt A.C.O. Morgan's party & especially the statement of No. 881 Cpl. Topp appended, it appears that the task of capturing the 3rd line of the Hostile Trenches - at any rate on the front allotted to the 4th Batt. Leicesters, was more | Appendix V |

LABEUVRIERE Oct. 13th (cont.)

serious than had been anticipated. And when Lt Morgan had ~~sat up his~~ caught up the main attack — he had left our trenches with the 4th line of the advance — it was already occupying the 2nd line trench in considerable numbers, but was unable to make any impression on the 3rd line.

Only one bomb could be fired from the trench mortar. After that the slow match or the firing charge refused to act.

Lt Morgan threw a certain number of bombs — less than 12, & then found the Infantry with only 1 officer left, & the men left without leaders.

He assisted this officer to collect a number of men lying down in the open behind the German 2nd line, & led them forward into the 2nd line, which seems to have been rather crowded already.

This one remaining officer was then killed, & Lt Morgan told the Infantry signallers to signal for reinforcements & according to one account — officers. Later on reinforcements are said to have come up — on the right.

Then Lt Morgan handed over the mortar to Corpl Turley & went into the trenches

LABEUVRIERE. i.e. the 2nd line trench, which was just
Oct. 13th (contd) in front of his mortar. It was about
about 10 minutes. As he left the trench, he
was heard to shout to the Infantry lying down
in shell holes behind the trenches. "Come
on 46th. You will never take this trench
today." Before he reached the detachment
he fell wounded, & died soon after in
the arms of Gr. Hawkins.

Soon after this the Infantry in the open
& some of those in the 2nd line trench fell
back, involving the trench mortar party,
who got separated. The mortar was stopped.
The bombs were carried back.

Later a 2nd advance was made, & Corpl
Insley & 2 men availed themselves of it
to endeavour to recover the mortar, but
cd not find it: nor Lt Morgan's body.
Most of the party remained in the trenches
all that night, & reported 1 by 1 next
day.

They reported that we were still holding the
1st & 2nd German lines when they left.

Casualties:-

Lt A.C.O. Morgan - killed.
Gr. Bolton - "
Gr. Gardner - wounded.
Dr. Burgoin - gassed by
a burst cylinder.

LA BEUVRIERE. Oct. 13th Oct. 14th. One man (Gr. Smith), of the ration party with Lt. Humphreys was wounded, not seriously.

Oct. 14th. Amm. Col provided a further ration party of 25 men for the trenches, & 25 men went from Batteries; while Lt. Adshead relieved Lt. Humphreys.

Oct. 17th. 2nd Lt. Adshead posted to this Brigade.

19th. Capt. Stirling, adjutant left to join the 25th Division & to take over command of C.84 Battery R.F.A.

20th. Lt. Col. Lemon from went to 46. D.A. & took command of D.A. during the absence of C.R.A., who went on leave.

21st. Lieuts Faber & Grimsham joined this Brigade from England, & were posted to (Amm. Col & 6th Batts respectively).

22nd. M.O. 2nd Lieut Ryder & Lt. Davies went on leave.

LA [illegible]VRIERE. Arrangements were made by XI Corps for
24th Oct. the Artillery of this Division to qualify
to relieve 18 pounder Batteries of 12th
& Guards Divn, now in position. This
was effected by sending detachments from
each battery to various batteries in
position. 3 shifts of 4 days were ordered.
This Brigade was linked with the
64th Bde. XII Division for this purpose.
The first shift went up today to the
Battery positions, which are near ANNEQUIN.
Amm. Col. moved billets to make room for Life Guards
2nd Lt. Charles Jewers joined this Bde.

26th. Lt. Col. [illegible] & Capt Worthley
visited Hqrs of 64th & 76th Brigades
at Annequin, with a view to above
scheme of reliefs being carried out.
Amm. Col. moved billets to make room
for Guards Infantry.

27th. Amm. Col. moved billets, & came to
rest at ~~Annezin~~ ANNEZIN.

28th. Details of the Div. Artillery, including
representative detachments of this Bde
were inspected by the King near ~~Foss~~
11 a.m. GOSNAY, as part of the XI Corps.

| | |
|---|---|
| 28. Oct. (cont^d) | After H.M. had inspected the IV Corps, [he] was thrown by his horse, frightened by the cheering, [illegible] & fell. The 46th Div. were therefore ordered not to cheer as H.M. drove away. |
| 30th Oct. | 2nd Lt. Harry [illegible] joined from England & was posted to Amm. Col. |

[illegible] Capt.
[illegible] 3 N.M. Bde. R.F.A.

46th Division

1/3rd N.M. Bde R.F.A.

Nov

Vol X

121
7694

Hmc

Confidential.

War Diary

of

3rd N M Bde RFA

from 1st to 30th November

1915.

~

LABEUVRIERE. Received orders that Indian Corps less 19th Division was leaving 1st Army & that XI Corps w.d be reconstituted as follows:- Guards, 19th & 46th Divns.
1st Nov.
Corps front to stretch from Givenchy northward to Fauquissart.
12th Divn. transferred to I Corps.

2nd Nov. Preliminary orders to move northward were to be in rear of line to be occupied. Divisional front to be from Cense COUR D'AVOUE northward to N. of NEUVE CHAPELLE.
5 Territorial & 1 S.R. battalions were to be attached to the Division.

4th Nov. Div. Artillery moved northward by Brigades via CHOCQUES - GONNEHEM - ROBECQ - LES AMUSOIRES to ST FLORIS. Left LABEUVRIERE 10.45 a.m. & arrived ST FLORIS 2.45 p.m.
One officer per Battery went forward & reconnoitred Battery positions of 4th Bde R.F.A. in MEERUT'S sector near RICHEBOURG ST VAAST. Appendix VI.
HQS. 3rd Brigade at house N of LA BASSEE Canal.
The march was much delayed at the outset by level crossings near Chocques.

St FLORIS.

5 November 8.30 a.m. — Received orders to stand by as disposition of batteries & reliefs w.d. be altered.

10.30 a.m. — Received orders that batteries of this Brigade w.d. relieve LAHORE Divn batteries, & not MEERUT Divn batteries. Hqrs w.d. be at BOUT DEVILLE, & w.d. relieve 11th Bde.

6th. — O.C. & B.C.s went up to 11th Bde HQS. & reconnoitred gun positions to be occupied later.

7th. — Bde HQS moved from billet to new billet at LA HAYE. S. of St FLORIS. Lt Col. Lemon [illegible] went to Hqrs R.A. and took over duties of C.R.A., Brig-Gen. Campbell having gone to Div. Hqrs as General of the Division, during the absence of the G.O.C. on leave.

8th–10th. — Reconnaissance of Battery positions & zones, with a view to the relief of the 11/12 & 12/13.

10th. — Capt. [illegible] went up to Bout Deville (11th Bde Hqrs) & then set

| | |
|---|---|
| St FLORIS. 10th November (contd) | . Lt Col. Tayn, who informed him that he had recd orders to take over the Left Group 46th D.A. until Lt Col. Lawson found his return. |
| | This group consists of 4th, 5th & 6th Staffs Batteries, & 1st Derby (How.) battery. |
| | Lt Col. Tayn therefore issued orders tonight to the above batteries dealing with (a) March from billets to the new posn. (b) Reliefs., founded on D. Art. O.O. No. 25, appended. |
| 11th 11.30 a.m. | Received orders to send 4th Battery condemned gun (no 1267) & 5th Batt. do (No.       ) to Bethune & exchange them for 2 new 15 pdr B.L.C. guns. |
| 1.15 p.m. | The Relieving column of Left Group, i.e. 1st Derby Batt. complete, 1 section of 4th Batt., ~~3~~ 5 Batt. less 1 gun, 6th Batt. complete, & 3 Amm Col. wagons marched out (Appendix VII) — Appendix VII. |
| 2 p.m. | Two condemned guns left, under Mr Hammond A.O.C. for Bethune, from 4th & 5th Batteries. The two new guns were transferred to the old carriages. Both were Mark IV. No. 1173 to 4th Battery, No. 1188 to 5th Battery. |

St. FLORIS. 12/11/15.

The remaining section of the 4th Battery marched up to BOUT DEVILLE in the afternoon, ~~leaving~~ and the Amm. Col. also went up & relieved the 11th Brigade Amm. Col. at PONT RIQUEUL, leaving only the Brigade Hqrs still out of action.

13/11/15.

Brigade Hqrs marched to BOUT DEVILLE & there relieved the 11th Bde. Hqrs, taking over the command of the Left Group of the 46th Division Artillery (~~[illegible]~~, which

10. a. m.

now passed to Lt. Col. Forge.

This group now consisted of 4th Staffs, 5th Staffs, & 6th Staffs. Batteries, together with the 1st Derby Batteries, & [illegible] covered a front extending from the place where the LA BASSÉE–ESTAIRES road cuts the enemy line, northwards to a point just about the centre of the W. side of BOIS DU BIEZ; this section of our trenches being occupied by the 137th Brigade, & forming the left flank of the Division.

On the left of the above group, reliefs had been proceeding, simultaneously with our own reliefs, by which part of the Lahore Divisional Artillery were replaced by Brigades of the Guards Div[l] Artillery.

And in order that the zone of the Left Group should be co-extensive with the trenches occupied by the 137 Inf. Bde, 2 of their field Batteries, viz. A/76 – Major Gardner-Waterman, & B/76 Capt. Browning – were allotted to the Left Group, & passed under the command of Lt Col. Forges. These 2 batteries were therefore given the zone immediately North of the zone referred to above & extending as far North as a road cutting the German trenches about 600 yds E.N.E. of Neuve Chapelle.

(see Div. Art. Prelim. Mem. ~~VIII~~ 12.11.15. App. VIII

14/11/15. The zones of A. & B. 76 as set out in appended Mems. were transposed, thus being the zones already registered.

Registration proceeded throughout the Group.

8 p.m. The 2nd & 3rd Lincs Batteries passed into the Left Group, as they were covering about 400 yards of trenches immediately S. of the La Bassée road, into which the 137th Bde had extended their front.

Communication was also established in case of need with the 26th Siege Batt. a 4 gun 60 pounder battery, so that

Heavy Artillery support could be called for if required. (Div. Art. O.O. No 26 appended) App VIII

15/11/15. 2.20 p.m. Enemy attempted some shelling of X roads south of Neuve Chapelle, known as Port Arthur, but the 5th Battery opening with their enfilade guns, this ceased.

The Indian Division from which we took over had recently made a great point of enfilade gun positions – detaching 1 gun for that purpose & posting it on a flank.

Note. Thus the 4th, 5th, A/76, B/76 & 2nd Lines batteries all took over enfilade gun positions, which appear to worry the enemy considerably, & cause them to reply wildly. Care is taken in placing these guns to screen their flashes from the side near the enemy, as they are generally posted fairly close to the trenches. Thus an intersection is rendered difficult.

2.45 p.m. The 2nd Lines enfilade guns caused a lot of hostile retaliation on [illegible] du Bois.

2nd Lt Sims & 2nd Lt Brodie joined the Brigade from England.

16/11/15. 10 a.m. Joint shoot at [illegible] 1st [illegible] Howitzers, & B/76 with H.E. The [illegible] was a mound just N. of Bois du Biez.

OUT DEVILLE . Enemy again whizz-banged our trenches. Organised retaliation was fired, & the enemy stopped.

17/11/15 All quiet until 12-45, when Huns again shelled our trenches. Three batteries were concentrated & retaliation fired. This policy was adhered to all through the afternoon.

5 p.m. Lt Col. Lemon Gower - returned from D.A. & took command of Left Group.

18/11/15 Things much quieter all the morning. About 3 p.m enemy searched for Hessians & nearly found 4th & 5th Batteries with 5.9 Hows. There was also some retaliation by us for whizz-bangs on our trenches & O.P.'s. But the latter was much less than on previous days.

19.11.15 - Things fairly quiet all day except for some whizz banging of our trenches, which was effectively silenced by our retaliation -

20.11.15 - 7.7's and one field battery fired on to the MUSK RAT in the

11.20 a.m. morning. Our batteries continued registering during the

| | |
|---|---|
| BOUTDEVILLE 20. 11. 15 (cont.) | day with the 2 18 pdr guns which arrived during the night previous to replace 15 pdrs. in each battery. Lt Col. Leveson Gower left to take over the duties of Temp. C.R.A. Major de Satgé took over duties of C.O. of the Brigade. |
| 21. 11. 15. | Enemy very active shelling our communication trenches and NEUVE CHAPELLE. Our batteries combined & retaliated effectively. |
| 22. 11. 15. | Day fairly quiet. At 4 p.m. the 2nd & 3rd Lancs Battery & 1st Derby Howitzer Battery left this group, and the batteries of 3rd Brigade & A76 switched on to new zones (in compliance with D.A.O.O. No 27.) App. IX |
| 23. 11. 15. | Two 18 pdr. guns arrived to each Battery the night previous to replace remaining 15 pdrs. Batteries were busy registering their new zones, but a large expenditure of ammunition provoked no |

| | |
|---|---|
| OUTTERSTEENE VILLE 23. 11. 15 (Cont.) | hostile fire. |
| 24. 11. 15. | A certain amount of hostile artillery fire about midday, which was however silenced by our fire. All quiet during the afternoon. Lt. J Anson returned from leave & took over the duties of adjutant. |
| 25. 11. 15. | Quiet during early part of the day. At 11.30 a.m. the enemy whizzbanged our front & support trenches in front of NEUVE CHAPELLE and the batteries of this group retaliated as usual in combination. At 1 p.m. a bombardment of the enemy's defences took place by the XIth Corps Artillery, assisted by part of the 46th D.A. (D.A.O.O. No 28) App. X. In accordance with this scheme the 4th Staffs. Battery opened fire at 1.15 p.m. firing 50 rounds at a slow rate. The other batteries stood to in readiness for expected reprisal, and were kept busy at intervals during the afternoon. |

26. 11. 15. The usual whizbanging of our trenches morning and afternoon, to which we responded as usual with a preponderance of ammunition. Out of 20 "crumps" fired by the enemy at noon into NEUVE CHAPELLE 5 were blind. An enemy sniper was very active during the day but was spotted by our infantry & hit when he left his post at dusk.

27. 11. 15. RUE DU BOIS was heavily crumped about 9.30 a.m., but after this hostile shelling was very slight all day, though our batteries were busy at intervals. A good deal of work appears to be going on in enemy's lines especially in neighbourhood of the ORCHARD.

28. 11. 15. A very quiet day. 6th Battery experimented in wirecutting. The guns were firmly anchored for the purpose & the shooting was reported as most accurate. In spite of the range (3400 yds) a decided amount of damage was done to the enemy's wire, which was

BOU[illegible] DE VILLE

28. 11. 15 (cont.) particularly thick at the point selected for the operation.

29. 11. 15. A certain amount of shelling from time to time all through the day. A few crumps fell near the 4th Battery position, but no damage done.

30. 11. 15. Hostile batteries very active during most of the day, & those of our group fired a large number of rounds in retaliation, particularly the 4th Staffs Battery. In the afternoon this battery's zone was very heavily whizbanged. Owing to the telephone wires being cut it was impossible to call on the neighbouring group batteries to assist us, & to thus maintain a superiority of fire over that of the enemy. Lt Colonel Leveson Gower returned from D.A. & took command of Left Group.

C. [illegible] Lt Col
Comdg 3 N M Bde RFA

CONFIDENTIAL.

--:--:--:--

WAR DIARY.

--:--:--:--

3rd: NORTH MIDLAND BRIGADE. R.F.A.

--:--:--:--:--:--

DECEMBER 1st: to 31st: 1915.

3rd NMBDE RFA    1    Hme

# WAR DIARY
*or*
~~INTELLIGENCE SUMMARY.~~
*(Erase heading not required.)*

Army Form C. 2118.

Instructions regarding War Diaries and Intelligence Summaries are contained in F. S. Regs., Part II. and the Staff Manual respectively. Title pages will be prepared in manuscript.

| Place | Date | Hour | Summary of Events and Information | Remarks and references to Appendices |
|---|---|---|---|---|
| BOUT DEVILLE | 1.12.15 | | 137th Infantry Brigade sent an early request for a quiet day, there was therefore practically no firing by our group batteries. Enemy were inactive except for a few whizbangs in afternoon, to which the 5th retaliated. A/76 Battery relieved by 'D' Battery R.H.A, who brought 3 guns (13 pdr) in action, one gun of A/76 being withdrawn. (D.A.O.O. No 29.) | App. XI |
| | 2.12.15 | | A good deal of artillery fire on both sides about midday. The batteries of 3rd Bde. had a small shoot at 3.30 pm. on enemy's communication trenches. | |
| | | 10.a.m. | Lt Colonel C. Leveson Gower went home on leave. Lt Colonel J. S. Ollivant RHA. took command of Left Group, and Major de Salzé of 3rd N.M. Brigade. | |
| | | 5.30pm. | The remaining 3 guns of 'D' Battery came into action, relieving the 3 guns of A/76. | |
| | | 10 pm. | A message arrived late in the evening stating that 46th Division would come out of action & be prepared to entrain (destination unknown) on night of Dec. 6-7. Officers on leave recalled. | |
| | 3.12.15 | | No firing by group batteries except a little registering by 'D' Battery. One section of each battery of the 3rd N.M. Brigade was relieved by a section of the 87th Brigade. The relieving unit took over our guns in exchange for those left in wagon lines at ST. VENANT, to which place our sections marched after being relieved. (D.A.O.O No 30.) All enfilade guns were taken over by C/86 Battery. All the relief arrived very late & our sections did not reach their billets till daylight on the following morning. | App XII |
| ST VENANT | 4.12.15 | 4pm. | Left Group Headquarters was relieved at 4pm. by 87th Brigade, and D.A. at the same hour. Remaining sections of our batteries relieved after dark and marched to billets at ST. VENANT. | |

Army Form C. 2118.

# WAR DIARY
*or*
~~INTELLIGENCE SUMMARY.~~
*(Erase heading not required.)*

Instructions regarding War Diaries and Intelligence Summaries are contained in F. S. Regs., Part II. and the Staff Manual respectively. Title pages will be prepared in manuscript.

| Place | Date | Hour | Summary of Events and Information | Remarks and references to Appendices |
|---|---|---|---|---|
| ST. VENANT | 5.12.15 | | Batteries spent the day overhauling guns. Ammunition Column relieved at 12 noon and joined the rest of Brigade at ST. VENANT. | |
| | | 8p.m. | Lt Colonel Leveson Power & Major Maxwell returned from leave. | |
| | | 10p.m. | Leave re-opened. 4th Battery man fell into LA BASSÉE Canal & was drowned. | |
| | 6.12.15 | | Lt Colonel C Leveson Power & Major Maxwell left again on leave. | |
| | 7.12.15 | | Sec. Lieuts H. S. Brodie. H. S. Foster and A. E. Sims posted to the Brigade to date from Dec. 6. | |
| | 8.12.15 | 11.a.m. | G.O.C. 46th Division inspected the Brigade dismounted in marching order. | |
| | 9.12.15 to 12.12.15 | | Nothing to record. | |
| | 13.12.15 | | Lt Colonel C. Leveson Power returned from leave. | |
| | 14.12.15 15.12.15 | | Nothing to record. | |
| | 16.12.15 | | Batteries marched out of billets as for embarkation & did 2 hours route march. | |
| | 17.12.15 18.12.15 | | Nothing to record. | |

1577 Wt. W10791/1773 500,000 1/15 D. D. & L. A.D.S.S./Forms/C. 2118.

3

Instructions regarding War Diaries and Intelligence Summaries are contained in F. S. Regs., Part II. and the Staff Manual respectively. Title pages will be prepared in manuscript.

# WAR DIARY
*or*
~~INTELLIGENCE SUMMARY.~~
*(Erase heading not required.)*

Army Form C. 2118.

| Place | Date | Hour | Summary of Events and Information | Remarks and references to Appendices |
|---|---|---|---|---|
| ST VENANT | 19.12.15 | | 46th Division moved into new area west of ST VENANT, 3 Bde did not move being already in the area —— | |
| | 20.12.15 to 22.12.15 | | Nothing to record | |
| | 23.12.15 | | Capt Wrottesley left this Bde and was attached to the D.A.C – | |
| | 24.12.15 | | Nothing to record – | |
| | 25.12.15 | | Xmas day, and was therefore as far as possible a holiday<br>Lt Adshead left on leave – | |
| | 26.12.15 | | One Section of 6th Battery and the Bde Ammunition Column moved into fresh billets E and SE of HOULERON<br>Lt Grimston left on leave – | |
| | 27.12.15 | | Lt Hickman left on leave – | |
| | 28.12.15 | | 2 Lt Sudlow ~~was~~ attached to this Brigade – | |
| | 29.12.15 | | 2 Lt Perkins ~~was~~ posted to this Brigade to date from 14th November 1915 – | |
| | 30.12.15 | | Lt Adshead returned from leave – | |
| | 31.12.15 | | Lt Grimston returned from leave – | |

Ch Gower Lt Col
Cmdg 3 N M. Bde RFA.

1577 Wt. W10791/1773 500,000 1/15 D. D. & L. A.D.S.S./Forms/C. 2118.

1/3 N M Bde R F A

Jan 1916

Vol XII

3rd N.M. Bde R.F.A.

Instructions regarding War Diaries and Intelligence Summaries are contained in F. S. Regs., Part II. and the Staff Manual respectively. Title pages will be prepared in manuscript.

# WAR DIARY

*or*

~~INTELLIGENCE SUMMARY.~~

*(Erase heading not required.)*

Army Form C. 2118.

| Place | Date | Hour | Summary of Events and Information | Remarks and references to Appendices |
|---|---|---|---|---|
| ST VENANT | 1.1.16 | | The following officers N C O's and men of this Bde were mentioned in despatches - Lt Col Leveson-Gower - Major C J Caddick - Capt Stirling - Capt Wolseley - Lt A C Morgan - Lt G V Stringer — No 1551 Sgt A Jones - No 1438 Bombdr W Rodgers - No 889 Bdr T W Vickery - No 202 Bombadier T W Waldron - Lt Ryder went on leave - | |
| | 2.1.16 | | Nothing to record | |
| | 3.1.16 | | Lt Faber went on leave | |
| | 4.1.16 to 5.1.16 | | Nothing to record | |
| | 6.1.16 | | Lt Heckman entrained at BERGUETTE with 13 men, 2 guns with limbers - | |
| | 7.1.16 | | Lt Munro went on leave - Lt Perkins returned from leave - Lt Davies entrained at BERGUETTE with 13 men, 2 guns with limbers - | |
| | 8.1.16 | | Nothing to record | |
| | 9.1.16 | | The remainder of this Bde, less horses and drivers, entrained at BERGUETTE and LILLERS. The detached party was left in charge of Capt T. Smith - Lt Ryder returned from leave - | APPENDIX No XIII |

1577 Wt. W10791/1773 500,000 1/15 D. D. & L. A.D.S.S./Forms/C. 2118.

Instructions regarding War Diaries and Intelligence Summaries are contained in F. S. Regs., Part II. and the Staff Manual respectively. Title pages will be prepared in manuscript.

# WAR DIARY
*or*
# INTELLIGENCE SUMMARY.
*(Erase heading not required.)*

Army Form C. 2118.

| Place | Date | Hour | Summary of Events and Information | Remarks and references to Appendices |
|---|---|---|---|---|
| between ST VENANT and MARSEILLE | 10.1.16 | | Lt Muras and Lt Faber returned to ST VENANT from Leave | |
| | to 11.1.16 | | Nothing to record – | |
| MARSEILLE | 12.1.16 | | This Brigade detrained at MARSEILLE and marched to Billets at POINT-ROUGE – | |
| | 13.1.16 | | Nothing to record – | |
| | 14.1.16 | | The following officers N.C.O's and men of this brigade were awarded the orders as given below to date from Jan 1st 1916 :– Lt Col. Leveson Gower a CMG – Lt G V Stringer a Military Cross – No 1250 Dr A Hawkins a D.C.M. No 2 Staff Sgt Wheeler F Lardner a D.C.M – No 861 Bdr G G Moore a D.C.M —— | |
| | 15.1.16 to 25.1.16 | | Nothing to record – | |
| | 26.1.16 | | The detached party entrained at BERGUETTE – The Brigade entrained at MARSEILLE | APPENDIX No XIV |

Instructions regarding War Diaries and Intelligence Summaries are contained in F. S. Regs., Part II. and the Staff Manual respectively. Title pages will be prepared in manuscript.

# WAR DIARY
*or*
~~INTELLIGENCE SUMMARY.~~

*(Erase heading not required.)*

Army Form C. 2118.

| Place | Date | Hour | Summary of Events and Information | Remarks and references to Appendices |
|---|---|---|---|---|
| PONT REMY | 27.1.16 | | The detached party detrained and marched to Billets at VAUCHELLE-Les DOMART | |
| | 28.1.16 | | The Brigade detrained and marched to Billets at VAUCHELLE-Les-DOMART | |
| VAUCHELLE LES DOMART | 29.1.16 to 31.1.16 | | Nothing to record | |
| | | | J.K.M. de Satgé Major<br>Cdg 3.N. Mid: Bde<br>R.F.A<br>31-1-16 | |

1577 Wt. W10791/1773 500,000 1/15 D. D. & L. A.D.S.S./Forms/C. 2118.

CONFIDENTIAL.

--:--:--

WAR DIARY.

--:--:--

3rd: NORTH MIDLAND BRIGADE. R.F.A.

--:--:--:--:--:--

FEBRUARY 1st: - 29th: 1916.

Vol XIII

97

2

# WAR DIARY
*or*
# ~~INTELLIGENCE SUMMARY.~~
*(Erase heading not required.)*

Army Form C. 2118.

Instructions regarding War Diaries and Intelligence Summaries are contained in F. S. Regs., Part II. and the Staff Manual respectively. Title pages will be prepared in manuscript.

| Place | Date | Hour | Summary of Events and Information | Remarks and references to Appendices |
|---|---|---|---|---|
| OUTREBOIS | 13.2.16 | | Major Lee left on Senior officers Course – | |
| | | | Lt Sims left on junior officers Course – | |
| | 14.2.16 | | Lt Colonel Leveson Gower left on leave – | |
| | 15.2.16 | | Major de Satgé took over duties of C.R.A – Major Meynell took command of the Brigade – | |
| | 16.2.16 | | Nothing to record – | |
| | 17.2.16 | | Lt Parker and Lt Cherry were attached to 4th N.M. Brigade RFA | |
| | | | Lt Kemp returned from leave – | |
| | 18.2.16 | | Major Lee returned from the Senior officers Course – | |
| | 19.2.16 | | Nothing to record – | |
| | 20.2.16 | | Major de Satgé left head quarters and went on a Senior officers Course | |

Instructions regarding War Diaries and Intelligence Summaries are contained in F. S. Regs., Part II. and the Staff Manual respectively. Title pages will be prepared in manuscript.

# WAR DIARY
*or*
# ~~INTELLIGENCE~~ SUMMARY.

(*Erase heading not required.*)

Army Form C. 2118.

Hmc

| Place | Date | Hour | Summary of Events and Information | Remarks and references to Appendices |
|---|---|---|---|---|
| VAUCHELLE LES DOMART | 1.2.16 to 4.2.16 | | Nothing to record | |
| | 5.2.16 | | Lt Keys went on leave | |
| | 6.2.16 to 8.2.16 | | Nothing to record | |
| | 9.2.16 | | Lt Holmes Lt Pope and Lt Ebery were attached to this Brigade from the 3/3 N.M. Brigade R.F.A | |
| | 10.2.16 | | Nothing to record | |
| | 11.2.16 | | Lt Parker was attached to this Brigade from the 3/3 N.M Brigade R.F.A<br>Lt Peaman Smith and five men went on leave | |
| | 12.2.16 | | The Brigade moved to OUTREBOIS – Colonel Leveson-Gower remained behind – Major de Satgé took Command of this Brigade | |

1577 Wt. W10791/1773 500,000 1/15 D. D. & L. A.D.S.S./Forms/C. 2118.

3

Instructions regarding War Diaries and Intelligence Summaries are contained in F. S. Regs., Part II. and the Staff Manual respectively. Title pages will be prepared in manuscript.

# WAR DIARY
*or*
# ~~INTELLIGENCE SUMMARY.~~
*(Erase heading not required.)*

Army Form C. 2118.

| Place | Date | Hour | Summary of Events and Information | Remarks and references to Appendices |
|---|---|---|---|---|
| OUTREBOIS | 21.2.16 | | Lt Evans and six men went on leave<br>Lt Pearman-Smith returned from leave – | |
| | 22.2.16 | | Nothing to record – | |
| | 23.2.16 | | Major Meynell Capt. Salt, Lt Ryder, Lt Adshead and Capt Pearman-Smith went up to ENGLEBELMER to reconnoitre gun positions, all except Major Meynell & Capt. Salt returned in the evening – | |
| | 24.2.16 | | Major Lee, Lt Anson, Lt Adshead and Lt Pearman-Smith went up to ENGLEBELMER to reconnoitre gun positions. Major Lee Capt Salt & Lt Anson returned in the evening – | |
| | 25.2.16 | | As many officers as could be spared were sent up to ENGLEBELMER to reconnoitre gun positions, all returning in the evening –<br>Lt-Colonel Leveson Gower returned from leave.<br>Major de Salis returned from Senior officers Course — | |

1577 Wt. W10791/1773 500,000 1/15 D. D. & L. A.D.S.S./Forms/C. 2118.

4

Instructions regarding War Diaries and Intelligence Summaries are contained in F. S. Regs., Part II. and the Staff Manual respectively. Title pages will be prepared in manuscript.

# WAR DIARY
*or*
# ~~INTELLIGENCE SUMMARY.~~
*(Erase heading not required.)*

Army Form C. 2118.

| Place | Date | Hour | Summary of Events and Information | Remarks and references to Appendices |
|---|---|---|---|---|
| OUTREBOIS | 26.2.16 | | Lt Colonel Leveson - Gower went to Head quarters to take over duties of CRA — | Brigade & Battery training were carried out during the Month |
| | 27.2.16 | | Lt Colonel Leveson - Gower returned from Head quarters | |
| | 28.2.16 | | Nothing to record | |
| | 29.2.16 | | Major Meynell Lt adorhead and Lt Pearman-Smith returned from Englebelmer — | |
| | | | C Leveson Gower Lt Col<br>Comdg 1/3 N. M. Bde RFA | |

CONFIDENTIAL

# WAR DIARY.

## 3rd: NORTH MIDLAND BRIGADE. R.F.A.

March 1st: to 31st: 1916.

Vol XIV

46

I

Instructions regarding War Diaries and Intelligence Summaries are contained in F. S. Regs., Part II. and the Staff Manual respectively. Title pages will be prepared in manuscript.

# WAR DIARY

*or*

~~INTELLIGENCE SUMMARY.~~

*(Erase heading not required.)*

Home

Army Form C. 2118.

| Place | Date | Hour | Summary of Events and Information | Remarks and references to Appendices |
|---|---|---|---|---|
| OUTREBOIS | 1.3.16 & 2.3.16 | | Nothing to record - | |
| | 3.3.16 | | Lt Munro returned from leave - | |
| | 4.3.16 & 5.3.16 | | Nothing to record - | |
| | 6.3.16 | | The Bde moved to MAZIERS - | |
| MAZIERS | 7.3.16 | | Head quarters Staff and battery Commanders moved to Mt St ELOY to take over from the French division and reconnoitre gun positions - | |
| | 8.3.16 | | The Bde moved up into action East of Mt St ELOY - also one Section of the 2nd Derby battery - Lt Sims returned from Gunnery Course | |
| Mt St ELOY | 9.3.16 | | Batteries registered their zones - the 4th on the right, 5th Centre, 6th left - Second Derby battery 2nd Section moved up into action - The Group wagon lines were at Acque | |

1577 Wt. W10791/1773 500,000 1/15 D. D. & L. A.D.S.S./Forms/C. 2118.

Instructions regarding War Diaries and Intelligence Summaries are contained in F. S. Regs., Part II. and the Staff Manual respectively. Title Pages will be prepared in manuscript.

1/3

# WAR DIARY

*or*

# ~~INTELLIGENCE SUMMARY~~

*(Erase heading not required.)*

Army Form C. 2118

| Place | Date | Hour | Summary of Events and Information | Remarks and references to Appendices |
|---|---|---|---|---|
| M^t S^t ELOY | 10·3·16 | 8 pm | Colonel Leveson-Gower assumed Command of Centre Group Consisting Of 2nd Derby Battery - 4th 5th 6th batteries — Covering 139th Infantry Brigade | |
| | 11·3·16 | | Wagons Lines moved to CAMBLAIN L'ABBE | |
| | 12·3·16 | | French Division on our right were attacked with gas - all quiet on our front - | |
| | 13·3·16 | | Enemy shelled the Bethune road our batteries retaliated otherwise nothing to report - | |
| | 14·3·16 | | 5th Battery were shelled no damage done though 60 shell were sent over - | |
| | 15·3·16 | | This village was shelled from 9 am to 2 pm no damage was done to this Brigade though some new troops in the village suffered very heavily - | |
| | 16·3·16 | | The Derby Battery & 6th Battery shot on mine Crater in 6th Battery zone many direct hits were obtained - but the 4·5 Howitzer was not large enough to destroy it - | |

1875 Wt. W593/826 1,000,000 4/15 J.B.C. & A. A.D.S.S./Forms/C. 2118.

3

Instructions regarding War Diaries and Intelligence Summaries are contained in F. S. Regs., Part II. and the Staff Manual respectively. Title Pages will be prepared in manuscript.

# WAR DIARY
*or*
# ~~INTELLIGENCE SUMMARY~~
*(Erase heading not required.)*

Army Form C. 2118

| Place | Date | Hour | Summary of Events and Information | Remarks and references to Appendices |
|---|---|---|---|---|
| M^T S^T ELOY | 17.3.16 | | Nothing to report during day - Major de Salze left for England to take Command of a new Brigade - | |
| | | 7pm | All batteries fired on C.T.s and roads behind German Lines - there was no retaliation - All repeated at 9.30 pm again no retaliation - | |
| | 18.3.16 | | Nothing to report during day - The 139 Bde re-adjusted it's line dividing the front into two sectors - | |
| | 19.3.16 | | Nothing to report | |
| | 20.3.16 | | The day passed quietly - the Sixth battery fired salvoes all through the night on Mine Crater in their Zone - | |
| | 21.3.16 } 22.3.16 } | | Light very bad both days ~~Capt Rambaut~~; ~~[illegible]~~ 15 men who signed on for the duration of the war, having served their five years, were granted leave on the 22nd 3.16 - Capt Rambaut went on leave - Colonel Leveson-Gower went to Head quarters to take over duties of C.R.A. - Major Meynell took Command of this Bde - 23.3.16. | |
| | 23.3.16 | | The 6th Battery had one man wounded while bringing rations up to gun position by railway — | |

1875 Wt. W593/826 1,000,000 4/15 J.B.C. & A. A.D.S.S./Forms/C. 2118.

4

Instructions regarding War Diaries and Intelligence Summaries are contained in F. S. Regs., Part II. and the Staff Manual respectively. Title Pages will be prepared in manuscript.

# WAR DIARY

*or*

# ~~INTELLIGENCE SUMMARY~~

*(Erase heading not required.)*

Army Form C. 2118

| Place | Date | Hour | Summary of Events and Information | Remarks and references to Appendices |
|---|---|---|---|---|
| M^t S^t ELOY | 24.3.16 | | Nothing to report | |
| | 25.3.16 | 12.30 am | Enemy sent up a mine on 4th Battery zone and occupied the Crater the 4th x 5th Batteries bombarded all doing some very useful firing on the Crater – we retook Crater but were driven out again at once – | |
| | | 8pm | 4th x 5th Batteries bombarded crater till daylight | App XV |
| | 26.3.16 | | Crater was bombarded all day x night by all Batteries firing salvoes into it every 15 minutes – Capt Salt x Lt Saint went on leave – | |
| | 27.3.16 | 1.30 am | western lip of crater was taken x held the 4 x 5th batteries bombarded CTs leading to the Crater till daylight giving infantry covering fire while they dug themselves in – 2Lt Crombie, 2Lt Steward, 2Lt Clark, 2nd Lt Winwood and 2Lt Goatman were attached to this Bde from the 3/3rd N of Bde. – 93 ORs reinforcements came up from base for D Battery, 25% of each ~~Battery~~ units gunners were sent to D Battery and reinforcements sent up to the other units to replace them – | " |
| | 28.3.16 | | Nothing to report | |
| | 29.3.16 | | day passed quietly – at 6pm a mine was sent up by 137 Bde on our right – All batteries assisted the right group by bombarding CTs on the right of our zone – | |

15/

# WAR DIARY
*or*
# INTELLIGENCE SUMMARY
*(Erase heading not required.)*

Army Form C. 2118

Instructions regarding War Diaries and Intelligence Summaries are contained in F. S. Regs., Part II. and the Staff Manual respectively. Title Pages will be prepared in manuscript.

| Place | Date | Hour | Summary of Events and Information | Remarks and references to Appendices |
|---|---|---|---|---|
| M^t S^t ELOY | 30.3.16 | | Lt Dumbell & 2nd Lt Barnaby were attached to this Bde from the 3rd/3rd N.M. Bde – day passed quietly – | |
| | 31.3.16 | | 2nd Lt Goatman & Winwood were attached to D.A.C. – day passed quietly – | |

Ch. Gower Lt. Col.
Commanding 3rd N Mid Bde R.F.A

1875 Wt. W593/826 1,000,000 4/15 J.B.C. & A. A.D.S.S./Forms/C. 2118.

CONFIDENTIAL

--:--:--

# WAR DIARY.

--:--:--

## 3rd: NORTH MIDLAND BRIGADE. R.F.A.

--:--:--:--:--:--

APRIL 1st: to 30th: 1916.

[redacted]

Vol 20

46

Instructions regarding War Diaries and Intelligence Summaries are contained in F. S. Regs., Part II. and the Staff Manual respectively. Title Pages will be prepared in manuscript.

# 1 WAR DIARY
*or*
~~INTELLIGENCE SUMMARY~~
*(Erase heading not required.)*

Hme

Army Form C. 2118

| Place | Date | Hour | Summary of Events and Information | Remarks and references to Appendices |
|---|---|---|---|---|
| Mt. St. ELOY | 1.4.16 | | Capt Rambaut returned from leave – | |
| | 2.4.16 | | Nothing to record – | |
| | 3.4.16 | | Major Lee and Lt Saint went on leave. Capt Salt and Lt Saint returned from leave – | |
| | 4.4.16 | | Lt Windle & Nicholls joined this Bde from the 3/3rd N M Bde RFA – | |
| | 5.4.16 | 6.45 pm | Mine went up on 4th Battery front our infantry occupied the Crater – | |
| | 6.4.16 | | Nothing to record – | |
| | 7.4.16 | | Capt P. Smith went on leave – Lt Saint was wounded while observing from our reserve trenches – | |
| | 8.4.16 | | Nothing to record – | |
| | 9.4.16 | | Lt Rowan returned from leave. Lt Col Leveson-Gower went to Senior Artillery officers Course – | |

1875 Wt. W593/826 1,000,000 4/15 J.B.C. & A. A.D.S.S./Forms/C. 2118.

Instructions regarding War Diaries and Intelligence Summaries are contained in F. S. Regs., Part II. and the Staff Manual respectively. Title Pages will be prepared in manuscript.

4th (2)

# WAR DIARY
or
~~INTELLIGENCE SUMMARY~~

*(Erase heading not required.)*

Army Form C. 2118

| Place | Date | Hour | Summary of Events and Information | Remarks and references to Appendices |
|---|---|---|---|---|
| Mt St ELOY | 10.4.16 | | A Strong point on 4th Battery zone was taken on by the heavies, TM's and the 4th Battery with very good results - Lt Col Gisborne took Command of the Centre Group - | |
| | 11.4.16 | | Major Meynell went on Leave also Lt Smith - | |
| | 12.4.16 | | Lt Keys left for England for a ranging Course - | |
| | 13.4.16 | | the 46th Div: Arty: fired on enemy CT.S, very little retaliation on our zone - All Leave was stopped — | |
| | 14.4.16 | | Lt Col Leveson-Gower returned from his Course and took Command of Centre Group - | |
| | 15.4.16 | | a Strong point ~~was~~ taken on by 6th Battery and 2nd Derby Battery Some very good direct hits were obtained, but the 4.5" howitzer was not Considered Large enough to do much damage — | |
| | 16.4.16 | | Capt P. Smith & Lt Sims returned from Leave - | |

1875 Wt. W593/826 1,000,000 4/15 J.B.C. & A. A.D.S.S./Forms/C. 2118.

Instructions regarding War Diaries and Intelligence Summaries are contained in F. S. Regs., Part II. and the Staff Manual respectively. Title Pages will be prepared in manuscript.

# WAR DIARY (4)
*or*
# INTELLIGENCE SUMMARY
*(Erase heading not required.)*

Army Form C. 2118

| Place | Date | Hour | Summary of Events and Information | Remarks and references to Appendices |
|---|---|---|---|---|
| MT ST ELOY | 24.4.16 | | The 4th and 5th Batteries were again shelled during the afternoon, a direct hit was obtained on No 2 Gun of 110th Bde in the 5th Battery position – The positions were cleared as soon as shelling started and there were no casualties —— | |
| | 25.4.16 | | A mine was blown up on 6th Battery front at 12 noon the enemy occupied the crater – 6th Battery fired on crater during afternoon – The remaining sections were relieved by the 110th Bde – | |
| | 26.4.16 | | A mine was blown up at 3am on left group zone we barraged the right of this zone till 5am with slow rate of fire – Lt Col Leveson Gower handed over command of Centre group to OC 110th Bde at 8am and marched with H.Q. Staff to new area – | |
| GOUY EN TERNOIS | 27.4.16 | | Lt Keys returned from his course – | |
| | 28.4.16 to 29.4.16 | | Lt Faber and Lt Adshead went on leave —— | |
| | 30.4.16 | | Lt Col. Leveson Gower went to hospital | J Megrell |

1875 Wt. W593/826 1,000,000 4/15 J.B.C. & A. A.D.S.S./Forms/C. 2118.

VI (3)

Army Form C. 2118

# WAR DIARY
*or*
# INTELLIGENCE SUMMARY
*(Erase heading not required.)*

Instructions regarding War Diaries and Intelligence Summaries are contained in F. S. Regs., Part II. and the Staff Manual respectively. Title Pages will be prepared in manuscript.

| Place | Date | Hour | Summary of Events and Information | Remarks and references to Appendices |
|---|---|---|---|---|
| Mt S: ELOY | 17.4.16 | | Two mines were blown up on our front by our infantry who occupied both craters – | app XVI |
| | 18.4.16 | | Major Meynell returned from leave also Lt Smith — | |
| | 19.4.16 | | The Centre group fired on Enemy CT's during the evening causing a large quantity of retaliation, an 8" was believed to have been in action – | |
| | 20.4.16 | | a mine was blown up on left group zone by the enemy, no help was asked for so we did not fire – | |
| | 21.4.16 | | Nothing to record | |
| | 22.4.16 | | Lt Heaton joined this Bde from 3rd/3rd N M Bde RFA – | |
| | 23.4.16 | | Lt Munas left for England for a range finding course – the 4th & 5th Batteries were shelled from 2.30pm to 3.30pm – 4 men were killed and two wounded Cpl Moore being one of the wounded died in hospital the next day – One section of each battery was relieved by sections of the 110th Bde | app XVII |

CONFIDENTIAL

--:--:--

# WAR DIARY.

--:--:--

232nd: BRIGADE. R.F.A.

late 1/3 N M Bde

--:--:--:--:--:--

May 1st: to 31st: 1916.

Vol 16

46

Instructions regarding War Diaries and Intelligence Summaries are contained in F. S. Regs., Part II. and the Staff Manual respectively. Title Pages will be prepared in manuscript.

# WAR DIARY I

*or*

~~INTELLIGENCE SUMMARY~~

*(Erase heading not required.)*

Hme Army Form C. 2118

| Place | Date | Hour | Summary of Events and Information | Remarks and references to Appendices |
|---|---|---|---|---|
| GOUY EN-TERNOIS | 1.5.16 | | Lt Smith was transferred to 2nd N.M. Bde RFA<br>Lt Grimston was transferred to 46 D.A.C – | |
| | 2.5.16 | | Lt Wenwood was posted to this Bde from D.A.C<br>Lt Hickman went on leave – | |
| | 4.5.16 | | D3 Battery drew their guns and battery wagons from St Pol also 83 L D horses – | |

1875 Wt. W593/826 1,000,000 4/15 J.B.C. & A. A.D.S.S./Forms/C. 2118.

Instructions regarding War Diaries and Intelligence Summaries are contained in F. S. Regs., Part II. and the Staff Manual respectively. Title Pages will be prepared in manuscript.

# WAR DIARY II
*or*
# ~~INTELLIGENCE SUMMARY~~
*(Erase heading not required.)*

Army Form C. 2118

| Place | Date | Hour | Summary of Events and Information | Remarks and references to Appendices |
|---|---|---|---|---|
| GOUY-EN-TERNAS. | 5/5/16 | | Lt Ryder & Lt Davies went on leave. | |
| | 6/5/16 | | Nothing to report | |
| | 7/5/16 | | Brigade moved to new billets at WARLINGCOURT | App |
| | 8/5/16 | | Lts Adshead & Faber returned from leave. | |
| WARLING-COURT | 9/5/16 | | C.R.A reconnoitred positions for 2 Batteries and a/C.O. showed them to B.C.s. | XVIII |
| | | | Lt Pearman Smith went on leave | |
| | 10/5/16 | | a/C.O reconnoitred positions for two Batteries to be lent to 37th Division | |
| | | | Work begun on 5th and 6th Battery positions | |
| | 11/5/16 | | 1 Section of 4th Battery and 1 Section of 3D Battery moved into action. | App XIX |
| | 12/5/16 | | a/C.O. with Signalling Officer reconnoitred route for buried cable. | |
| | | | Lt Hickman returned from leave. | |
| | 13.5.16 | | Nothing to report | |
| | 14.5.16 | | Lt Keys and Lt Heath went on leave – | |
| | 15.5.16 | | Lt Ryder and Lt Davies returned from leave – | |

1875 Wt. W593/826 1,000,000 4/15 J.B.C. & A. A.D.S.S./Forms/C. 2118.

Instructions regarding War Diaries and Intelligence Summaries are contained in F. S. Regs., Part II. and the Staff Manual respectively. Title Pages will be prepared in manuscript.

# WAR DIARY III
*or*
~~INTELLIGENCE SUMMARY~~
*(Erase heading not required.)*

Army Form C. 2118

| Place | Date | Hour | Summary of Events and Information | Remarks and references to Appendices |
|---|---|---|---|---|
| WARLINCOURT | 16.5.16 and 17.5.16 | | Nothing to report - | |
| | 18.5.16 | | Lt Foster went on leave - Lt Faber was posted to "C" Battery - Lt Clark became orderly officer - | |
| | 19.5.16 | | Lt Peaman-Smith returned from leave - | |
| | 20.5.16 | | The Bdes of the 46 Div Arty ~~were renumbered~~ 230, 1, 2, 3, - This Bde being 232nd Bde - Batteries were Called A B C D respectively — | |
| | 21.5.16 | | ~~Nothing to report~~ - "C" Battery relieved "D" Battery | |
| | 22.5.16 | | Lt Steward went on a junior Artillery ~~School~~ Course<br>Lt Heaton went on a trench Mortar Course<br>Lt Perkins went on leave<br>The Bde ammunition column was transferred with Lt Winwood his personnel and horses shown in app to XX — | app XX |
| | 23.5.16 | | D Battery 232nd Bde was transferred to the 233rd Bde<br>D (How) " 233rd " " " " 232nd Bde | app XX |

1875 Wt. W593/826 1,000,000 4/15 J.B.C. & A. A.D.S.S./Forms/C. 2118.

Instructions regarding War Diaries and Intelligence Summaries are contained in F. S. Regs., Part II. and the Staff Manual respectively. Title Pages will be prepared in manuscript.

# WAR DIARY
or
# INTELLIGENCE SUMMARY
*(Erase heading not required.)*

Army Form C. 2118.

| Place | Date | Hour | Summary of Events and Information | Remarks and references to Appendices |
|---|---|---|---|---|
| 22-5-16 to 23-5-16 | | | Re-organization. The Ammunition Columns.<br>Batteries were completed with men from the B.A.C. prior to it being transferred to D.A.C.<br>All officers of the B.A.C. were posted to Batteries before transfer, except Lieut Winwood who was transferred to D.A.C. with the remainder of B.A.C.<br>Horses. Batteries were complete with L.D. Horses, Also one Officers Charger and 13 Riding Horses were transferred from the B.A.C before re-organization.<br>Batteries. 3D Battery was transferred to the 233rd Brigade RFA complete. 2nd Derby Battery was transferred to this Brigade complete.<br>———<br>'B' Battery have had trouble during the month with mange with our Horses. | |
| | 6-5-16 | | Colonel C. Hewson. Gowen. C.G.S. struck off strength. | |

Maxwell Major
232 Bde RFA

2449 Wt. W14957/M90 750,000 1/16 J.B.C. & A. Forms/C.2118/12.

CONFIDENTIAL

--:--:--

WAR DIARY.

--:--:--

HEAD QUARTERS

232nd: BRIGADE. R.F.A.

--:--:--:--

JUNE 1st: to JUNE 30th: 1916.

@@@@@@@@@@@@@@@@@@

Instructions regarding War Diaries and Intelligence Summaries are contained in F. S. Regs., Part II. and the Staff Manual respectively. Title Pages will be prepared in manuscript.

# WAR DIARY
*or*
# INTELLIGENCE SUMMARY
*(Erase heading not required.)*

Army Form C. 2118.

Hmc

| Place | Date 1916. | Hour | Summary of Events and Information | Remarks and references to Appendices |
|---|---|---|---|---|
| WARLINCOURT | June 1st | | Major Meynell went to LUCHEREZ (UX) to witness practice attack. | |
| | 2nd | | C.O and Adjutant spend the day going round Gun Positions and O.P.s. Medical Office proceeded on leave. Lt Fraser took the duties of Medical Officer while Capt Armitage was on leave | |
| | 3rd | | Lieut J. Ebery went on leave. | |
| | 3rd | | GOC, CRA and ADVS inspected 'B' South Staffs Battery Horses and came to the conclusion they should be isolated and that all Nose bags, Hay-nets, Grooming Kit and Blankets should be destroyed, all Horses and Harness to be washed thoroughly and men to be disinfected. | |
| | 3rd | | Capt. G. M. Rambaut was attached to R.F.C as observer. | |
| | 3rd | | Major H. V. B. De Satge awarded D.S.O. | |
| | | | No 1529 B.S.M. Males H. awarded D.C.M | |
| | 4th | | CO and Adjutand witnessed practice attack 5 AM. at LUCHEUX | |
| | 5th | | C.O. and two Battery Commanders witnessed practice attack at LUCHEUX | |
| | 5th | | One section of 'A' and 'C' South Staffs Bty were relieved by Batteries of the 125th Brigade, RFA | |
| | 6th | | Remaining section of 'A' & 'B' South Staffs Battery were relived by 125th Brigade, RFA. | |

2449 Wt. W14957/M90 750,000 1/16 J.B.C. & A. Forms/C.2118/12.

Army Form C. 2118.

# WAR DIARY
*or*
# INTELLIGENCE SUMMARY
*(Erase heading not required.)*

Instructions regarding War Diaries and Intelligence Summaries are contained in F. S. Regs., Part II. and the Staff Manual respectively. Title Pages will be prepared in manuscript.

| Place | Date | Hour | Summary of Events and Information | Remarks and references to Appendices |
|---|---|---|---|---|
| WARLINCOURT | June 6th | 1916. | Disinfecting of 'B' South Staffs Battery Horses and Harness was comenced | |
| | 7th | | Disinfecting of 'B' South Staffs Battery Horses was completed | |
| | 8th | | New Clothes for 'B' South Staffs Battery and Grooming material arrived, all old Grooming Material was burnt also Nose-bags and Haynets | |
| | 9th | | 'B' South Staff Battery infected clothes were sent to 139th Brigade, Headquarters LUCHEUX to be disinfected. | |
| | 10th to 12 | | Bad weather hindered the Work at Gun Positions | |
| | " | | Major H. L. Newton returned from Leave | |
| | 10th | | Owing to the large quantities of R.E. Material still required the D.A.C. lent 18 G.S. Wagons to the Brigade. These Wagons were horsed by Units to which they were allotted, and Ammunition for Gun Positions was delivered by the D.A.C. to the Guns in the D.A.C. Limbered Ammunition Wagons | App 21 |
| | | | Orders received to maintain the following percentage 18 Pdr Ammunition 60% A 40% AX. For wire cutting Batteries 75% A. 25% AX | |
| | 10th | | Lieut E. R. Mewas attached to 3rd Army T.M. School | |

Instructions regarding War Diaries and Intelligence Summaries are contained in F. S. Regs., Part II. and the Staff Manual respectively. Title Pages will be prepared in manuscript.

# WAR DIARY
*or*
# ~~INTELLIGENCE SUMMARY~~
*(Erase heading not required.)*

Army Form C. 2118

| Place | Date | Hour | Summary of Events and Information | Remarks and references to Appendices |
|---|---|---|---|---|
| WARLINCOURT | 24.5.16 | | Batteries of this Bde were named A B C (South) Stafford Batteries, D (Derby) Battery – | |
| | 25.5.16 | | Lt Barnaby went on an anti aircraft Course – | |
| | 26.5.16 | | Lt Munas went on leave. Lt Heath returned from leave – | |
| | 27.5.16 to 29.5.16 | | Nothing to report | |
| | 30.5.16 | | Major Newton went on leave | |
| | 31.5.16 | | Nothing to report | |

J Wezwell
Major
Cmdg – 232nd Bde R.F.A

1875 Wt. W593/826 1,000,000 4/15 J.B.C. & A. A.D.S.S./Forms/C. 2118.

Army Form C. 2

Instructions regarding War Diaries and Intelligence Summaries are contained in F. S. Regs., Part II. and the Staff Manual respectively. Title Pages will be prepared in manuscript.

# WAR DIARY
*or*
# INTELLIGENCE SUMMARY
*(Erase heading not required.)*

| Place | Date | Hour | Summary of Events and Information | Remarks and references to Appendices |
|---|---|---|---|---|
| | | | "D" Derby Battery return Horses lent to them by other Batteries for Riding School and Grooming purposes. | |
| 12-3-16 to 31-3-16. | | | All Batteries worked on Gun Positions and Dug-outs behind FONQUEVILLERS these were a new pattern brought out by the VII. Corps as Shell-proof, all Dug-outs being 14 feet below the ground and the Gun-pits having Two roofs to them.<br>These dug-outs of course used an enormous amount of Material (i.e.) large Timber and Cement which meant an extra quantity of transport.<br>Wagons were borrowed from the D.A.C. for this purpose and as many as 23 G.S. Wagon loads were taken from the R.E's dump MONDICOURT to the Gun Positions. in one night<br>The 'B' Battery's position was nearly completed by the end of the month.<br>'D' Derby Battery's position was already made but not the new pattern as it was considered the position to be well hidden.<br>'A' and 'C' Batteries position on the other hand were very backward owing to the two Batteries being in action with the 37th Division making it impossible for them to do any work on it themselves.<br>25 Infantry men per Battery were lent to these Batteries for the purpose of digging.<br>The R.E's assisted in building all positions.<br>OP's in front FONQUEVILLERS. were commenced by all Batteries enfilade Gun Positions were chosen and commenced by 'A' and D. Battery. Trenches were commenced for Telephone Wires which under the new idea were all to be buried 6 feet deep. | |

2449 Wt. W14957/M90 750,000 1/16 J.B.C. & A. Forms/C.2118/12.

Army Form C. 2118.

# WAR DIARY
*or*
# INTELLIGENCE SUMMARY
*(Erase heading not required.)*

Instructions regarding War Diaries and Intelligence Summaries are contained in F. S. Regs., Part II. and the Staff Manual respectively. Title Pages will be prepared in manuscript.

| Place | Date 1916 | Hour | Summary of Events and Information | Remarks and references to Appendices |
|---|---|---|---|---|
| | June 11th | | Batteries commenced to fill their Ammunition Dumps at Gun Positions. | |
| | 12 to 16th | | During this period work was carried on at the Gun Positions 18 to 20 loads of R.E. Material was taken up nightly, Dump at Gun Positions were completed to 1000 rds 18 Pdr 700 rds. 4.5 Hows. Fatigue parties consisting of reinforcements and men from Headquarters Staff construct Brigade Headquarters and some Trenches in front of SOUASTRE. Corpl Rollo and 2 Telephonists layed and Poled telephone line to Batteries | |
| | 14th | | Lieut F R Heaton attached to T M School | |
| | 15th | | Capt. W. S. Pearman-Smith and B.S.M. Thomas were mentioned in dispatches. 2Lieut H. O. Barnaby 'C'/S.S. Battery posted 25th Anti Aircraft Battery vice Lieut W. H. Pender auth VIII Corps A/64 5/565 dated 17/4/16 | |

2449 Wt. W14957/M90 750,000 1/16 J.B.C. & A. Forms/C.2118/12.

Army Form C. 2118.

# WAR DIARY
*or*
# INTELLIGENCE SUMMARY
*(Erase heading not required.)*

Instructions regarding War Diaries and Intelligence Summaries are contained in F. S. Regs., Part II. and the Staff Manual respectively. Title Pages will be prepared in manuscript.

| Place | Date | Hour | Summary of Events and Information | Remarks and references to Appendices |
|---|---|---|---|---|
| | 1916 | | | |
| In Front of SOUASTRE | June 17th | | C/SS Battery went into action 3 Guns, A/SS Battery went into action, Both just West of FONQUEVILLERS. Wagon ~~Lines~~ lines moved to GAUDIEMPRE. Brigade Headquarters moved to Dug-outs just in front of SOUASTRE. | App. 22 |
| | 17th | | Medical Officer returned from leave. | |
| | 18th | | This Brigade was attached to Left Group. 46th Division for all tactical purposes. Left Group commanded by Lieut. Col. Sir Hill Child Bart MVO. DSO. | |
| | 19th | to 23. | During this Period Batteries registered and completed their Gun Positions and OPS. and OP exchange behind FONQUEVILLERS was dug and put into working order. | |
| | 24th | | U days Bombardment commenced. | App. 23 |
| | | | Major E B Lee evacuated CCS sick. Capt. E J Salt took command of B/SS Battery. Light varying from good to bad, showery all day. Retaliation feeble except in our Trenches | |
| | ~~20th~~ 25th | | V. Days Bombardment was carried out. ~~appendix~~ No weather + observation same as U Day. 3 Balloons were brought down by our [illegible] Aircraft, Retaliation feeble except in our Trenches. | App 23 |
| | 26. | | W. Days Bombardment was carried out weather, light and observation same as V Day. | |
| | | | Capt F. M Rambaut wounded. Lt J G Anson took command of A/SS Battery. Lt Spurrier sent to Hospital (Sick) | |

2449 Wt. W14957/M90 750,000 1/16 J.B.C. & A. Forms/C.2118/12.

Army Form C. 2118.

Instructions regarding War Diaries and Intelligence Summaries are contained in F. S. Regs., Part II. and the Staff Manual respectively. Title Pages will be prepared in manuscript.

# WAR DIARY
*or*
# INTELLIGENCE SUMMARY

*(Erase heading not required.)*

| Place | Date | Hour | Summary of Events and Information | Remarks and references to Appendices |
|---|---|---|---|---|
| In Front of SOUASTRE | 1916 June 29th | | Y Days Bombardment was carried out. | app 23 |
| | 30. | | Lieut F Heaton went to Hospital Sick | |
| | | | Y Days Bombardment was carried out | |
| | | | During the whole weeks Bombardment the retaliation was very feeble both on Gun Positions and Trenches. | |
| | | | Very poor weather through-out the whole of the Bombardment except the last day. | |

2449 Wt. W14957/M90 750,000 1/16 J.B.C. & A. Forms/C.2118/12.

CONFIDENTIAL.

--:--:--

WAR DIARY.

--:--:--

232nd: BRIGADE. R.F.A.

--:--:--:--:--

July 1st: to July 31st: 1916.

@@@@@@@@@@@@@@@

Instructions regarding War Diaries and Intelligence Summaries are contained in F. S. Regs., Part II. and the Staff Manual respectively. Title Pages will be prepared in manuscript.

# WAR DIARY
*or*
# INTELLIGENCE SUMMARY
*(Erase heading not required.)*

Army Form C. 2118.

Rmc

| Place | Date | Hour | Summary of Events and Information | Remarks and references to Appendices |
|---|---|---|---|---|
| Just in front of SOUASTRE | July 16. 1st | | "Z" Days bombardment was carried out. Zero commencing at 7-30 AM. First news received that the attack had been successful, but afterwards news was received that the Staffords were held up in Front of GOMMECOURT WOOD. | App F.6.1 |
| | | | The 139th Brigade, 5th and 7th Battns were seen in the 2nd German line after the smoke which lasted for 1 hour had cleared away. it appeared that the first 3 or 4 waves got straight through to the 2nd line the last few waves seemed to have been caught by the Germans coming out in great force from their deep dug-outs in the front line. Thus cutting off the first 4 waves. | |
| | | | The 137th Brigade were held up entirely in front of GOMMECOURT WOOD and never reached the German 1st line Trench. | |
| | | | 2Lt. T A M Davies and Lieut E. H. L. Clark. who went over with the 139th Brigade were either killed or captured. | |
| | | | The 56th Division obtained their objective, but were driven back the following evening, and the line of 46th and 56th Division remained in the same position as it was before the Bombardment commenced. | |
| | | | Major F. H. Meynell acted as Liaison Officer to 139th Brigade, Headquarters throughout the attack. | |
| | 2nd | | The day passed quietly, nothing to report. | |
| | 2nd | | Major C. A. Lee and Lieut J. Z. [illegible] evacuated. Auth. 46 Div. A2532/24. | |

2449 Wt. W14957/M90 750,000 1/16 J.B.C. & A. Forms/C.2118/12.

Instructions regarding War Diaries and Intelligence Summaries are contained in F. S. Regs., Part II. and the Staff Manual respectively. Title Pages will be prepared in manuscript.

# WAR DIARY
*or*
# INTELLIGENCE SUMMARY
*(Erase heading not required.)*

Army Form C. 2118.

| Place | Date | Hour | Summary of Events and Information | Remarks and references to Appendices |
|---|---|---|---|---|
| In front of SOUASTRE | 1916 July. 3rd | | a portion of the line slightly north | app F161 |
| | | 4pm | one section of Batteries of 282nd Bde was relieved by one section of Batteries from 280th Brigade (Stripped Guns). Personnel of three sections relieved sections of Batteries of 125th Brigade then in position. | |
| | 3rd | | German observation Balloon brought down by our aircraft. | |
| | 4th | 12 noon | Remaining sections of this Brigade were relieved by personnel of Batteries of 280 Brigade. | |
| | | 6pm | The C.O. and B.C.s handed over command to 56th Division | |
| | 4th | | During the afternoon it rained heavily for about 2 hours flooding out all dug-outs and Ammunition dumps damaging a large proportion of the ammunition dumped at the Gun Position | |
| BIENVILLERS. | 5th | 6am | The Brigade took over from the 125th Brigade. The day passing quietly, nothing to report | |
| | 6th to 9th | | Nothing to report | |
| | 10th | | Personnel of 1 section of Batteries of 123rd Brigade relieved Personnel of 1 section of this Brigade | |

2449 Wt. W14957/M90 750,000 1/16 J.B.C. & A. Forms/C.2118/12.

Army Form C. 2118.

Instructions regarding War Diaries and Intelligence Summaries are contained in F. S. Regs., Part II. and the Staff Manual respectively. Title Pages will be prepared in manuscript.

# WAR DIARY
or
# INTELLIGENCE SUMMARY

(Erase heading not required.)

| Place | Date | Hour | Summary of Events and Information | Remarks and references to Appendices |
|---|---|---|---|---|
| | July 16 | | | |
| BIENVILLERS | 11th | | Remaining section of 123rd Brigade relieve one section of this Brigade | |
| | | | C.O and B.C's handed over command to 123rd Brigade, and the Brigade Headquarters marched to BASSEUX | |
| In front of BEAUMETZ | 11th | | 'A' Battery went into action just in front of Beaumetz. | |
| | 12th to 14th | | The days passing quietly nothing to report. | |
| S of BERLES | 15th | | 'B' & 'C' Battery went into action just S of BERLES, one section of 'D' Battery went into action in BIENVILLERS under Right Group. 'A' Battery and left section of 'D' Battery remaining in the Centre Group. Brigade Headquarters BC & D Battery Wagon lines moved to LA CAUCHIE | app. F.17 |
| | 15th | | Lieut P.B. Pearman-Smith took over Townmajorship of LA CAUCHIE | |
| | 20th | | Field obtained for Driving Drill for use of 'B' 'C' & D Batteries. 'A' Battery unable to use the field owing to distance of Wagon lines. | |
| | 20th to 31st | | Nothing to report. | |

J. Lazell
Lt Col
232 Bde RFA

CONFIDENTIAL.

--:--:--:--

WAR DIARY.

--:--:--

232nd: Brigade. R.F.A.

--:--:--:--

AUGUST 1st: to AUGUST 31st: 1916.

@@@@@@@@@@@@

Army Form C. 2118.

Instructions regarding War Diaries and Intelligence Summaries are contained in F. S. Regs., Part II. and the Staff Manual respectively. Title Pages will be prepared in manuscript.

# WAR DIARY
*or*
# INTELLIGENCE SUMMARY
*(Erase heading not required.)*

Mmc

| Place | Date 1916 | Hour | Summary of Events and Information | Remarks and references to Appendices |
|---|---|---|---|---|
| LA CAUCHIE | 31-7-16 | | 2/Lieut F. R. Heath 'A' Battery attached to Artillery School as assistant Instructor. | |
| " | " | | Lieut. D. R. Viscount Sandon "B" Battery went on Course with Divisional Artillery School | |
| " | " | | 2/Lieut. N. C. Crombie 'C' Battery went on Course with Divisional Artillery School. | |
| " | 1-8-16 | | 2/Lieut. C. R. Muras 'C' Battery Posted to Y46 Trench Mortar Battery. | |
| " | " | | Lieut. F. W. Cave joined Brigade | |
| " | 2-8-16. | | No 642 Dr Wootton H. 'D' Battery awarded Military Medal. | |
| " | " | | No 988 Bombdr Whetstone J. A. awarded Military Medal | |
| " | 5-8-16 | | Lieut G. V. Faber rejoined 'C' Battery after course with Artillery School | |
| " | 6-8-16. | | Lieut. F. R. Heath struck off Strength | |
| " | " | | Capt. C. J. Salt 'B' Battery went on Course at 3rd Army Artillery School. | |

Instructions regarding War Diaries and Intelligence Summaries are contained in F. S. Regs., Part II. and the Staff Manual respectively. Title Pages will be prepared in manuscript.

# WAR DIARY
*or*
# INTELLIGENCE SUMMARY
*(Erase heading not required.)*

Army Form C. 2118.

| Place | Date | Hour | Summary of Events and Information | Remarks and references to Appendices |
|---|---|---|---|---|
| LA CAUCHIE | 6-8-16 | | Lieut H. D. Ryder, Headquarters Staff, took over the duties of Town Major LA CAUCHIE vice Lieut P. B. Pearman-Smith. | |
| | 8-8-16 | | 2/Lieut H. Leafe "B" Battery went on Course at 2" Trench Mortar School. | |
| | 9-8-16 | | 2/Lieut. N. Giblin attached to Brigade from X 36 T. M. Battery. | |
| | 10-8-16 | | Capt F. R. Armitage, R.A.M.C. attached to 43 CCS for Hospital Duties. | |
| | " | | Lieut Fitzgerald R.A.M.C. took over duties of Medical Officer of Brigade | |
| | 14-8-16 | | Lieut D. R. Viscount Sandon Rejoins "B" Battery after course at Artillery School. | |
| | " | | 2/Lieut H. Leafe Rejoins "B" Battery after course at 2" Trench Mortar School. | |
| | " | | 2/Lieut N. C. Crombie rejoins 'C' Battery after course at 46th Div. Arty. School | |
| | 15-8-16 | | 2/Lieut S. H. Burra "D" Battery went on course at 46th Div Arty School. | |
| | " | | Lieut C. E. Hickman went on Artillery course. | |

Instructions regarding War Diaries and Intelligence Summaries are contained in F. S. Regs., Part II. and the Staff Manual respectively. Title Pages will be prepared in manuscript.

# WAR DIARY
*or*
# INTELLIGENCE SUMMARY
*(Erase heading not required.)*

Army Form C. 2118.

| Place | Date 1916 | Hour | Summary of Events and Information | Remarks and references to Appendices |
|---|---|---|---|---|
| LA CAUCHIE | 16-8-16 | | Lieut A. E. Sims struck off strength upon posting to A.S.C. Horse Transport. | |
| " | " | | 2/Lieut F. Middleton attached to Brigade. | |
| " | " | | 2/Lieut H. J. Bednall posted to 'C' Battery. | |
| " | 17-8-16 | | Lieut Colonel F. H. Meynell Headquarters Staff went to 3rd Army Artillery School on Course. | |
| " | 17-8-16 | | The construction of Horse Standings for Brigade was commenced under the supervision of Lieut F. Heaton. Eight G S Wagons were lent to the Brigade for the transport of material for Horse Standings. | |
| " | 19-8-16 | | Major Lee C.B. joined Brigade after evacuation | |
| " | 18-8-16 | | Major C.B. Lee took over Command of Brigade during the absence of Lt. Colonel F. H. Meynell. | |

2449 Wt. W14957/M90 750,000 1/16 J.B.C. & A. Forms/C.2118/12.

Instructions regarding War Diaries and Intelligence Summaries are contained in F. S. Regs., Part II. and the Staff Manual respectively. Title Pages will be prepared in manuscript.

# WAR DIARY
*or*
# INTELLIGENCE SUMMARY
*(Erase heading not required.)*

Army Form C. 2118.

| Place | Date | Hour | Summary of Events and Information | Remarks and references to Appendices |
|---|---|---|---|---|
| LA CAUCHIE | 21-8-16 | | Sports were held by this Brigade at LA CAUCHIE including a jumping competition open to all Officers of the Division. | |
| " | 28-8-16 | | Commencement of Reorganization. half Right section of C/232 Battery transferred to A/232 Battery. | app No CRA 772 |
| | | | Half left section of C/232 Battery transferred to B/232 Battery. | |
| | 29-8-16 | | Remaining half-sections of C/232 were transferred to A/232 and B/232 Battery's respectively | app CRA 772 |
| POMMIER | 29-8-16 | 4pm | Brigade Headquarters took over command of Right Group | app. CRA 772 |
| | " | | Lieut Colonel L. G. Gisborne C.M.G. transferred from 233. Brigade to Command 232nd Brigade RFA | |
| | " | | 2Lieut A. F. Dufton 233 Brigade Transferred to 232 Brigade | |
| | " | | Major F. J. Wrottesley C/232 Battery Transferred to D/230 Brigade. | |
| | " | | Capt. W. S. Pearman-Smith C/233 Brigade transferred to 232 Brigade | |

2449 Wt. W14957/M90 750,000 1/16 J.B.C. & A. Forms/C.2118/12.

Instructions regarding War Diaries and Intelligence Summaries are contained in F. S. Regs., Part II. and the Staff Manual respectively. Title Pages will be prepared in manuscript.

# WAR DIARY
*or*
# INTELLIGENCE SUMMARY
*(Erase heading not required.)*

Army Form C. 2118.

| Place | Date | Hour | Summary of Events and Information | Remarks and references to Appendices |
|---|---|---|---|---|
| POMMIER | 29/8/16. | | Lieut. C. E. Hickman Returned from Artillery Course | |
| | " | | Capt G.D. Wilson Transferred from 233 Brigade to 232 Brigade | |
| | " | | Lieut. J. M. Joyce Transferred from 233 Brigade to D/232 Brigade | |
| | " | | Lieut. S. H. Burra D/232 Battery rejoined unit from Artillery Course. | |
| | " | | Right Group Bombardment carried out in accordance with OO 18 | app. 0085 |
| | 30/8/16. | | Capt. G. McRambaut Rejoined A/232 Battery after evacuation to England. | |
| | " | | Lieut. T. W. Cave To Div Arty School on Course | |
| | " | | Lieut. M. S. Windle To Divisional Artillery School on Course | |
| | " | | Right Group Bombarded German Trenches, Infantry reported Wire was not sufficiently cut. Wire not being cut enough Infantry Raiding party did not start. | R.O.O 18. |

Lionel Colone
Lieut Colonel
Commdg. 232nd Brigade, R.F.A.

2449 Wt. W14957/M90 750,000 1/16 J.B.C. & A. Forms/C.2118/12.

W A R D I A R Y.

August - 1916

APPENDIX - C.R.A.772.

-:-:-:-:-:-:-:-:-:-:-

28th:/ 29th: AUGUST.

Re,organization of Divisional Artillery.

Owing to orders having been received that all 18 Pdr: Batteries should be turned into 6 Gun Batteries instead of 4, and no extra Guns being given to the Division to do it with, the 232nd Brigade was turned into two-6-Gun Batteries, and one Battery of 4 Howitzers instead of three 4 Gun 18 Pdr Batteries and one Battery of 4 Howitzers.

This necessitated one 18 Pdr: Battery being split up.

Orders were received from Headquarters, Divisional Artillery, that "C" Battery, or the old 6th: Staffs Battery must be split up, which was done accordingly.

Major F.J.WROTTESLEY, the B.C, being transferred to 230th: Brigade, to Command a Battery, Lieut. G.V.FABER and Lieut.T.W.CAVE transferred to A/232 Battery with the Right Section - Lieut.N.C.CROMBIE and Lieut. C.E.HICKMAN being transferred to B/232 Battery with the Left Section.

All surplus Stores, Vehicles and Harness were returned.

The 233rd Brigade being split up between the 230th: and 231st: Brigades to complete them to three 18 Pdr: Batteries, which left the 232nd Brigade with the Headquarters of the/233rd: Brigade. old

Personnel and Horses of which were sent to "D" Battery, surplus Vehicles and Stores being returned to Ordnance.

Lieut. Colonel L.G.GISBORNE.C.M.G. was posted to the Command of the re-organized 232nd Brigade, and Lieut. A.F.DUFTON was posted as Orderly Officer.

Temporary Lieut. Col.F.H.MEYNELL, relinquished the rank of Lieut. Colonel and again took Command of "A" 232 Battery.

Temporary Capt. J.G.ANSON, relinquished his rank of Capt. and remained with "A"232 Battery.

Lionel Gisborne

Lieut. Colonel.

5.9.16. Commanding 232nd Brigade R.F.A.

CONFIDENTIAL.

--:--:--

# WAR DIARY.

--:--:--

232nd: Brigade. R.F.A.

--:--:--:--

SEPTEMBER 1st: to SEPTEMBER 30th: 1916.

--:--:--:--

Vol 20

Instructions regarding War Diaries and Intelligence Summaries are contained in F. S. Regs., Part II. and the Staff Manual respectively. Title Pages will be prepared in manuscript.

# WAR DIARY
*or*
# ~~INTELLIGENCE SUMMARY~~

*(Erase heading not required.)*

(1)

Army Form C. 2118.

| Place | Date | Hour | Summary of Events and Information | Remarks and references to Appendices |
|---|---|---|---|---|
| | 1.9.16 | | Nothing to report | |
| POMMIER | 2.9.16 | | 137 infantry Bde raided the enemy's line capturing 4 prisoners and killing 15 germans, The centre group covered the party with great success, assisted by the right Group – | app XXIX |
| | 3.9.16 | | 2 Lieut Middleton went to hospital sick otherwise nothing to report | |
| | 4.9.16 | 9.30 pm | Trench mortars bombarded Salient W23(a) x W24(a) ref RANSART 1/10,000 A/232 Battery assisted with covering fire – | app XXX |
| | 5.9.16 | 10 pm to 10.30 pm | Enemy's trench Railways and dumps were bombarded, There was no retaliation – otherwise nothing to report – | app XXXI |
| | 6.9.16 | | 2nd Lt Windle rejoined from Divisional School – day passed quietly nothing to report – | |
| | 7.9.16 | | 2nd Lts Edwards, Windle, Tristy and Chatfield were ~~were~~ posted to 56th Division – otherwise nothing to report | |
| | 8.9.16 | | 2nd Lt Leafe posted to Trench Mortars | |

2449 Wt. W14957/M90 750,000 1/16 J.B.C. & A. Forms/C.2118/12.

Instructions regarding War Diaries and Intelligence Summaries are contained in F. S. Regs., Part II. and the Staff Manual respectively. Title Pages will be prepared in manuscript.

# WAR DIARY
*or*
# ~~INTELLIGENCE SUMMARY~~
*(Erase heading not required.)*

(2)

Army Form C. 2118.

| Place | Date | Hour | Summary of Events and Information | Remarks and references to Appendices |
|---|---|---|---|---|
| POMMIER | 9.9.16 | 2 am | Gaps were cut in Enemy's wire at four places on the right group front; 18pdr Batteries fired on enemy's front and support lines. The wire was cut by means of gas pipes charged with ammonal; The 18pdr fire objective was to kill Germans who were alarmed by the explosions and who had come out of their dug outs to man their trenches – | app XXXII |
| | | 4pm to 5pm | A232 and B232 gave covering fire for the trench mortars, firing at irregular intervals on the enemy's front and support trenches The 91st Siege Battery (9.2) engaged Monchy Church at the same time – | app XXXIII |
| | 10.9.16 | | Nothing to report | |
| | 11.9.16 | | Ten other ranks (Surplus) were posted to the D.A.C. – | |
| | 12.9.16 | | RSM Blines returned from a months leave – | |
| | 13.9.16 14.9.16 | | Nothing to report | |
| | 15.9.16 | | Major Meynell went on leave | |
| | 16.9.16 | | ~~2nd Lt Middleton returned from hospital~~ | |
| | 17.9.16 | | Major Newton and Capt. Rambaut went on an artillery course (3rd army) | |

Instructions regarding War Diaries and Intelligence Summaries are contained in F. S. Regs., Part II. and the Staff Manual respectively. Title Pages will be prepared in manuscript.

# WAR DIARY
*or*
# INTELLIGENCE SUMMARY
*(Erase heading not required.)*

(3)

Army Form C. 2118.

| Place | Date | Hour | Summary of Events and Information | Remarks and references to Appendices |
|---|---|---|---|---|
| POMMIER | 18.9.16 | | Nothing to report | |
| | 19.9.16 | | Capt Pearson-Smith went to the 41st Division to take Command of a battery – | |
| | 20.9.16 | | Nothing to report | |
| | 21.9.16<br>22.9.16 | | This group extended its front to E 28 Central taking over the zone of the Northern group of the 33rd Division. LX D232 relieved D230 A231 moving further South, The group then became the Centre group composed of A232, A231, B232, and D232. 2nd Lt Pearson Smith went to Hospital – | app XXXIV |
| | 23.9.16<br>24.9.16 | | Nothing to report – | |
| | 25.9.16 | | Major Meynell returned from leave otherwise nothing to report | |
| | 26.9.16<br>27.9.16<br>28.9.16 | | Nothing to report | |

Army Form C. 2118.

# WAR DIARY
*or*
# ~~INTELLIGENCE SUMMARY~~
*(Erase heading not required.)*

(4)

Instructions regarding War Diaries and Intelligence Summaries are contained in F. S. Regs., Part II. and the Staff Manual respectively. Title Pages will be prepared in manuscript.

| Place | Date | Hour | Summary of Events and Information | Remarks and references to Appendices |
| --- | --- | --- | --- | --- |
| POMMIER | 29.9.16 | | Enemy shelled FONQUEVILLERS between 6pm and 7pm This group retaliated on ESSARTS, otherwise day passed quietly – | |
| | 30.9.16 | | Enemy Trench Mortars were very active both day and night from MONCHY direction our batteries engaged them each time they opened fire – otherwise nothing to report – | |
| | | | [illegible] Lt Col<br>Cmdg 233 Bde RFA | |

2449 Wt. W14957/M90 750,000 1/16 J.B.C. & A. Forms/C.2118/12.

CONFIDENTIAL.

--:--:--

# WAR DIARY.

--:--:--:--

232nd: BRIGADE. R.F.A.

--:--:--

October 1st: to October 31st: 1916.

**********

Vol 21

Army Form C. 2118.

Instructions regarding War Diaries and Intelligence Summaries are contained in F. S. Regs., Part II. and the Staff Manual respectively. Title Pages will be prepared in manuscript.

# WAR DIARY
*or*
# ~~INTELLIGENCE~~ SUMMARY
*(Erase heading not required.)*

(1)

| Place | Date | Hour | Summary of Events and Information | Remarks and references to Appendices |
|---|---|---|---|---|
| TOMMIER | 1.10.16 } 2.10.16 } | | Nothing to report | |
| | 3.10.16 | | Lt Crombie went on leave | |
| | 4.10.16 | | Nothing to report | |
| | 5.10.16 | | The 138 Bde carried out a raid on Enemy's lines near MONCHY, the trenches were entered @ 11.30pm on finding no trace of life in Enemy's lines they returned one officer and one O.R. were slightly wounded – The Centre group gave covering fire to Trench Mortar bombardment during the afternoon, B/232 cutting two gaps in enemy's wire, also during the afternoon – Bombardment of Enemy's trenches was also carried out during the raid – | app XXXV |
| | | | The 230 Bde came to TOMMIER taking part of there Bde head quarters – | |
| | | | A/231 and the ~~4~~ right section D232 started making new positions West of FONQUEVILLERS | |

2449 Wt. W14957/M90 750,000 1/16 J.B.C. & A. Forms/C.2118/12.

Instructions regarding War Diaries and Intelligence Summaries are contained in F. S. Regs., Part II. and the Staff Manual respectively. Title Pages will be prepared in manuscript.

# WAR DIARY
or
# ~~INTELLIGENCE~~ SUMMARY
(Erase heading not required.)

Army Form C. 2118.

(2)

| Place | Date | Hour | Summary of Events and Information | Remarks and references to Appendices |
|---|---|---|---|---|
| POMMIER | 6.10.16 | | A/231 left this group coming under the 33rd Division - B/232 extended its zone to the point of the By Z being the Southern Limit of new zone for centre group - RX D/232 went to a new position west of FONQUEVILLERS | app XXXVI |
| | 7.10.16 | | Nothing to report | |
| | 8.10.16 | | Enemy shelled BERLES doing very little damage considering the length of time they shelled | |
| | 9.10.16 | | at 10 am this group shortened its line the Southern most point being E11d69 (Fonquevillers 1/10,000) | ~~app XXXVII~~ |
| | 10/10/16<br>11/10/16 | | Nothing to report except A/232 detached section and D/232 were badly shelled | |
| | 12/10/16 | | A combined bombardment with Stokes Mortars and divisional artillery (18 pdr) was carried out during the night; no retaliation from the enemy - | app XXXVIII |
| | 13.10.16 | | Major Newton and Capt Rambaut returned from artillery course | Lt Combes returned from leave |
| | 14.10.16 | | On both the 13th and 14th BERLES was very heavily shelled all the morning. A/232 detached section moving to new position at W14d3070 during the night of 13/14th | |

2449 Wt. W14957/M90 750,000 1/16 J.B.C. & A. Forms/C.2118/12.

Instructions regarding War Diaries and Intelligence Summaries are contained in F. S. Regs., Part II. and the Staff Manual respectively. Title Pages will be prepared in manuscript.

# WAR DIARY
*or*
# ~~INTELLIGENCE SUMMARY~~
*(Erase heading not required.)*

(3)

Army Form C. 2118.

| Place | Date | Hour | Summary of Events and Information | Remarks and references to Appendices |
|---|---|---|---|---|
| TOMMIER | 15·10·16 16·10·16 | | Nothing to report except Major Lee & Capt Harlam went to 3rd Army Artillery School | 15/10/16 |
| | 17·10·16 | | A/231 and RX D 232 rejoined this group, which then became right group covering from E11b 55·30 to W23d 94·45 (MONCHY Salient – | app XXXVIII |
| | 18·10·16 | | The 138 infantry Bde raided enemy's lines in two places at 8·30pm returning at 9·5pm, with one German Helmet and a few other trophies suffering very few casualties themselves. The Centre group gave covering fire to trench Mortars during the afternoon, and assisted the raid by placing an effective box barrage on trenches East of the two points of entry | app XXXIX |
| | 19/10/16 | | Capt Armitage returned from attachment at 43 CCS | |
| | | | A 232 and D 232 did much damage to Enemy's new work in W29B – | |
| | 20/10/16 | | Nothing to report – | |
| | 21/10/16 | | 2nd Lt Perkins went on a Third army heavy trench Mortar Course – | |
| | 22/10/16 | | Lt Nichols was transferred to a unit in England | |
| | | | Lt Burra took over duties of Town Major La CAUCHIE – | |

2449 Wt. W14957/M90 750,000 1/16 J.B.C. & A. Forms/C.2118/12.

Instructions regarding War Diaries and Intelligence Summaries are contained in F. S. Regs., Part II. and the Staff Manual respectively. Title Pages will be prepared in manuscript.

# WAR DIARY

*or*

~~INTELLIGENCE SUMMARY~~

*(Erase heading not required.)*

(4)

Army Form C. 2118.

| Place | Date | Hour | Summary of Events and Information | Remarks and references to Appendices |
|---|---|---|---|---|
| TOMMIER | 23/10/16 – 25/10/16 | | Nothing to report | |
| | 26/10/16 | | Capt Salt went on leave | |
| | 27/10/16 | | Colonel Gisborne went on leave Major Meynell took Command of right group – D 512 4.5 howitzer Battery joined this Bde Commanded by Capt Houghton and was met by the adjutant at Doullens Station at 5am – Lieut Donavan and 2Lt's White Agar and Anderson also came with D512 Battery – | |
| | 28/10/16 | | 2nd Lt Perkins returned from trench mortar School | |
| | 29/10/16 | | Lt Anson & 2Lt Arkwright went to Divisional Artillery School | |
| | 30/10/16 | | One Sub Section of D 512 was attached to D/230 and one Subsection to D/231, for instruction; two Subsections to D232 for the same purpose – Major Kent took Command of right group | |
| | 31/10/16 | | Nothing to report | |

Meynell Major for Lt Col
Cmdg 232 Bde RFA

2449 Wt. W14957/M90 750,000 1/16 J.B.C. & A. Forms/C.2118/12.

Secret.

~~CONFIDENTIAL~~

WAR DIARY

232ND. BRIGADE, R.F.A.

November 1916.

Vol 22

Instructions regarding War Diaries and Intelligence Summaries are contained in F. S. Regs., Part II. and the Staff Manual respectively. Title Pages will be prepared in manuscript.

# WAR DIARY
*or*
# INTELLIGENCE SUMMARY
*(Erase heading not required.)*

232nd Bde. (1)
RFA 46 Div.

Army Form C. 2118.

| Place | Date | Hour | Summary of Events and Information | Remarks and references to Appendices |
|---|---|---|---|---|
| TOMMIER | 1/11/16 2/11/16 | | Nothing to report | |
| | 3/11/16 | | Enemy put 4 4.2 gun shells into TOMMIER doing no damage; One of our aeroplanes came down in Enemy's lines at about 3.55pm B/232 gave our a airman time to get clear then fired 40 rounds rapid into area where the plane fell- | |
| | ~~4/11/16~~ | | D/512 Battery given the name of C/232, sent one section into action with D/232 RX and their other section went into action with D/231 | app 210 |
| | 4/11/16 | 4.35pm | Hostile aeroplane dropped two bombs into BIENVILLERS doing no damage, otherwise nothing to report- | |
| | 5/11/16 | | M G R A went round right group OPs | |
| | 6/11/16 | | Tommier was shelled | |
| | 7/11/16 | | ditto one civilian killed two soldiers wounded | |
| | 8/11/16 | | no damage done | |
| | 9/11/16 | | Lt Colonel Gisborne and Capt Salt returned from leave D/232 and A/231 engaged a 77mm Battery located in the South of ADINFER Wood - Enemy shelled our tracks round BIENVILLERS we retaliated on tracks E of MONCHY – | |

2449 Wt. W14957/M90 750,000 1/16 J.B.C. & A. Forms/C.2118/12.

Instructions regarding War Diaries and Intelligence Summaries are contained in F. S. Regs., Part II. and the Staff Manual respectively. Title Pages will be prepared in manuscript.

# WAR DIARY
or
~~INTELLIGENCE SUMMARY~~
*(Erase heading not required.)*

232 nd Bde (11) RFA. 46th Div.

Army Form C. 2118.

| Place | Date | Hour | Summary of Events and Information | Remarks and references to Appendices |
|---|---|---|---|---|
| TOMMIER | 10/11/16 | | Enemy again shelled our tracks round BIENVILLERS we again retaliated on the MONCHY tracks otherwise nothing to report | |
| | 11/11/16 }<br>12/11/16 } | | Nothing to report | |
| | 13/11/16 | 2.40 am | gass was discharged from our left sector ~~—~~ the enemy's trenches & tracks were shelled C/232 left the right group LX D/232 moved to RX D/232 BIENVILLERS RX D/230 joined this group - otherwise nothing to report | app 42 |
| | 14/11/16 | | Nothing to report | app 41 |
| | 15/11/16 | | Nothing to report | |
| | 16/11/16 | | Bombardment of enemy tracks + tramways | app 43 |
| | 17/11/16 | | Nothing to report concerning ~~[illegible]~~ operations Lieut H.D. RYDER proceeded to 46 Divisional Artillery school for course. Lieut F.M. Joyce rejoined Brigade from VII corps H.Q and took over duties of adjutant Vice Lieut RYDER on course. | |
| | 18/11/16 | | Nothing to report | |
| | 19/11/16 | | Right group 46 Divisional artillery becomes Left Group 48 Divisional artillery, and is composed of A/231 B/232 D/232 | app 44 |

2449 Wt. W14957/M90 750,000 1/16 J.B.C. & A. Forms/C.2118/12.

Instructions regarding War Diaries and Intelligence Summaries are contained in F. S. Regs., Part II. and the Staff Manual respectively. Title Pages will be prepared in manuscript.

# WAR DIARY
*or*
# INTELLIGENCE SUMMARY
*(Erase heading not required.)*

232nd (111) Bde RFA 46 Div: Army Form C. 2118.

| Place | Date | Hour | Summary of Events and Information | Remarks and references to Appendices |
|---|---|---|---|---|
| POMMIER | 20.11.16 | | Nothing to report | |
| | 21.11.16 | | Enemy shelled the vicinity of BIENVILLERS | |
| | 22.11.16 | | Nothing to report | |
| | 23.11.16 | | Enemy attempted to raid Y Sector all batteries fired on S.O.S lines | |
| | 24.11.16 | | A/231 doing wire cutting for projected raid on enemy trenches | app 45 |
| | 25.11.16 | | Projected raid cancelled. Received orders as to relief of Group by Left Group 49 divisional Arty | app 46 |
| | 26.11.16 | | One Section A/231 and B/232 relieved by Sections of A/245 and B/245 and went into action A/231 at R13C 7.6. B/232 at W3C 8.0. One Section D/232 relieved by one section D/245 and proceeded to Wagon lines | |
| | 27.11.16 | | Remaining Sections A/231 and B/232 relieved by remaining Sections A/245 and B/245 and went into action A/231 at one gun R13 D 83.08 two guns Q18 D 90.10 one gun R13 C 7.6 B/232 at W3C 8.0 and W14 D 14.75 Remaining Section D/232 relieved by remaining Section D/245 and proceeded to Wagon Lines H.Q. relieved by H.Q. 245 Bde RFA and proceeded to LA CAUCHIE | |

2449 Wt. W14957/M90 750,000 1/16 J.B.C. & A. Forms/C.2118/12.

Army Form C. 2118.

Instructions regarding War Diaries and Intelligence Summaries are contained in F. S. Regs., Part II. and the Staff Manual respectively. Title Pages will be prepared in manuscript.

# WAR DIARY
*or*
# INTELLIGENCE SUMMARY
*(Erase heading not required.)*

232 Bde. (IV) R.F.A. 46 Div.

| Place | Date | Hour | Summary of Events and Information | Remarks and references to Appendices |
|---|---|---|---|---|
| LACAUCHIE | 28.11.16 | | Nothing to report. | |
| | 29.11.16 | | Received VII Corps Order No 49 re Bombardment | |
| | 30.11.16 | | Received orders re relief of 46 Divisional artillery by 30th Division artillery Group and Battery commanders of relieving group came over to view positions etc VII Corps Corps order 49 postponed. | app 47 and 48 |

Lionel Colone Lt Col
Commdg 232 Brigade R.F.A.

2449 Wt. W14957/M90 750,000 1/16 J.B.C. & A. Forms/C.2118/12.

Secret

CONFIDENTIAL.

--:--:--

WAR DIARY.

--:--:--

232nd: Brigade. R.F.A.

--:--:--:--

December 1st: to December 31st: 1916.

Vol 23

Instructions regarding War Diaries and Intelligence Summaries are contained in F. S. Regs., Part II. and the Staff Manual respectively. Title Pages will be prepared in manuscript.

# WAR DIARY
*or*
# ~~INTELLIGENCE SUMMARY~~
*(Erase heading not required.)*

(1)

Army Form C. 2118.

| Place | Date | Hour | Summary of Events and Information | Remarks and references to Appendices |
|---|---|---|---|---|
| LA CAUCHIE | 1/12/16 | | Lt Ryder rejoined Bde from Div. Arty. Course - 1st Section of Batteries moved to new area - 2 Lt Birch joined this Bde | |
| | 2/12/16 | | Nothing to report | |
| | 3/12/16 | | Bde HQ and the remaining Sections of the Batteries moved to GROUCHES having been relieved by 149 Bde | app 49 |
| GROUCHES | 4/12/16 | | Nothing to report Batteries spent the day cleaning up Billets etc | |
| | 5/12/16 | | Batteries practised the march past in the morning and again in the afternoon as a Brigade | |
| | 6/12/16 | | GOC presented medal ribbons to the Div Arty the following belonged to this Bde:- No 1294 Corpl ROLLO. W.C., No 919 Corpl. WALKER. J., No 1202 Corpl. WALDRON. L.V., No 1350 Bomdr GLOVER. C.H., No 1844 Private FRYER. W.J. (RAMC attached). The following were not at the G.O.C's parade, but have been awarded the "Military Medal" No 1449 Sergt STOKES. F.W., No 889 Sergt. VICKERY. T.W., No 872 Bomdr ROBINSON A.H. | app 50 |
| | | | The following officers joined this Bde:- 2/Lieutenant D. CHIPPENDALE, 2/Lieutenant W. C. HANSON, 2/Lieutenant A. H. LEVY. (LEVY) | |
| | 7/12/16 | | Batteries started training - working party of 1 officer and 10 OR's of B/232 Battery went up to "IOMMIER" to prepare gun position | ~~app 51~~ app 51 |

2449 Wt. W14957/M90 750,000 1/16 J.B.C.&A. Forms/C.2118/12.

Instructions regarding War Diaries and Intelligence Summaries are contained in F. S. Regs., Part II. and the Staff Manual respectively. Title Pages will be prepared in manuscript.

# WAR DIARY
*or*
~~INTELLIGENCE~~ SUMMARY
*(Erase heading not required.)*

(2)

Army Form C. 2118.

| Place | Date | Hour | Summary of Events and Information | Remarks and references to Appendices |
|---|---|---|---|---|
| GROUCHES | 8/12/16 | | Nothing to report | |
| | 9/12/16 | | Two Sections of B/232 went into action NE of POMMIER their wagon lines at PAS | App 51 |
| | 10/12/16 | | B/232 ammunition wagons and teams returned to GROUCHES as there was no accommodation for them at PAS | |
| | 11/12/16 } 12/12/16 } | | Nothing to report | |
| | 13/12/16 | | The GOCRA gave a lecture on "Discipline" Lt Ryder went on leave - | |
| | 14.12.16 | | Nothing to report | |
| | 15.12.16 | | Nothing to report | |
| | 16.12.16 | | Brigade field day. all batteries on parade with skeleton staff. A and D batteries gave Christmas dinners to men. | |

2449 Wt. W14957/M90 750,000 1/16 J.B.C. & A. Forms/C.2118/12.

Instructions regarding War Diaries and Intelligence Summaries are contained in F. S. Regs., Part II. and the Staff Manual respectively. Title Pages will be prepared in manuscript.

# WAR DIARY
*or*
~~INTELLIGENCE SUMMARY~~

*(Erase heading not required.)*

(3)

Army Form C. 2118.

| Place | Date | Hour | Summary of Events and Information | Remarks and references to Appendices |
|---|---|---|---|---|
| GROOCHES | 17. 12. 16. | | C.R.A gave a lecture to officers and N C O^s on employment of Artillery. Received orders re relief of 49 Divisional artillery by 46^th Divisional artillery | app 52 |
| | 18. 12. 16 | | Brigade and Battery commanders proceeded to H Q 247 Bde RFA at BIENVILLERS to reconnoitre battery positions | |
| | 19. 12. 16 | | Nothing to report | |
| | 20. 12. 16 | | One Section of all batteries relieved one Section of all batteries of 247 Bde R.F.A | |
| | 21. 12. 16 | | Remaining Section of all batteries relieved remaining Sections of 247 Bde R.F.A Brigade Commander took over command of line at 12 Noon HQ at BIENVILLERS. | |

2449 Wt. W14957/M90 750,000 1/16 J.B.C. & A. Forms/C.2118/12.

Instructions regarding War Diaries and Intelligence Summaries are contained in F. S. Regs., Part II. and the Staff Manual respectively. Title Pages will be prepared in manuscript.

# WAR DIARY
*or*
# ~~INTELLIGENCE SUMMARY~~
*(Erase heading not required.)*

Army Form C. 2118.

(4)

| Place | Date | Hour | Summary of Events and Information | Remarks and references to Appendices |
|---|---|---|---|---|
| BIENVILLERS | | | | |
| | 22.12.16 | | Lieut C.H. ARKWRIGHT proceeded on Short leave to ENGLAND. Lieut HICKMAN and Lieut ANSON rejoined Brigade from 3rd Army Artillery School. | |
| | 23.12.16 | | C.R.A Commenced daily conference at Bde H.Q. | |
| | 24.12.16 | | Nothing to report | |
| | 25.12.16 | | Nothing to report | |
| | 26.12.16 | | Lieut J.G. ANSON proceeded on short leave to ENGLAND | |
| | 27.12.16 | | Lieut H.D. RYDER returned from leave | |
| | 28.12.16 | | Enemy attempted to raid the trenches on the front of the group on our right between 3 and 4 A.M. Major B LEE proceeded to ENGLAND for course at LARKHILL | |
| | 29.12.16 | | Nothing to report | |

2449 Wt. W14957/M90 750,000 1/16 J.B.C. & A. Forms/C.2118/12.

Instructions regarding War Diaries and Intelligence Summaries are contained in F. S. Regs., Part II. and the Staff Manual respectively. Title Pages will be prepared in manuscript.

# WAR DIARY
*or*
# ~~INTELLIGENCE SUMMARY~~
*(Erase heading not required.)*

(5)

Army Form C. 2118

| Place | Date | Hour | Summary of Events and Information | Remarks and references to Appendices |
|---|---|---|---|---|
| BIENVILLERS | | | | |
| | 30.12.16 | | Nothing to report | |
| | 31.12.16 | | Nothing to report | |

Frank Partome Lt Col
Commdg 232 Brigade RFA

1875 Wt. W593/826 1,000,000 4/15 J.B.C. & A. A.D.S.S./Forms/C. 2118.

CONFIDENTIAL.

--:--:--

WAR DIARY.

--:--:--

232nd: BRIGADE. R.F.A.

--:--:--

JANUARY 1st: to JANUARY 31st: 1917.

**********

Vol 24

Instructions regarding War Diaries and Intelligence Summaries are contained in F. S. Regs., Part II. and the Staff Manual respectively. Title Pages will be prepared in manuscript.

# WAR DIARY
*or*
# ~~INTELLIGENCE SUMMARY~~
*(Erase heading not required.)*

(1)

Army Form C. 2118

| Place | Date | Hour | Summary of Events and Information | Remarks and references to Appendices |
|---|---|---|---|---|
| BIENVILLERS | | | | |
| 1.1.17 | | | Major MEYNELL and Captain ARMITAGE RAMC awarded the D.S.O. BSM A SAYER awarded the D.C.M. Authority London Gazette New Years Honors 1917. | |
| 2.1.17 | | | Reorganisation of artillery commenced C/232 being split up right Section being transferred to D/230 left Section to D/231, Captain HOUGHTON, 2/Lts ANDERSON and AGAR being posted to D/231 Lieut DONOVAN and 2/Lt WHITE being posted to D/230. Lieut A.F. DUFTON Proceeded on leave | app 53 |
| 3.1.17 | | | C/247 Batty posted to 232 Bde R.F.A and relieved B/232 Batty in action, B/232 taking up a new position West of FONQUEVILLERS, one Section D/247 Batty posted to D/232 Batty. D/232 Batty took over position of old C/232 Batty.<br>The following officers were posted to this Brigade from 247 Bde R.F.A<br>Major W. HOWSON<br>Captain A.H. HAYNES<br>Lieut. S. J. BLAKE<br>2/Lieut G.D. BRUNTON.<br>2/Lieut T.R. IBBETSON<br>2/Lieut S. HARVEY.<br>a portion of 46 DAC and a portion of 49 DAC were transferred to this Brigade to form a Bde ammunition column with the following officers<br>The Brigade now consists of A, B, C Batteries (6 18 Pdrs) D Battery (6 4.5" Hows) and Ammunition column | |

1875 Wt. W593/826 1,000,000 4/15 J.B.C. & A. A.D.S.S./Forms/C. 2118.

Instructions regarding War Diaries and Intelligence Summaries are contained in F. S. Regs., Part II. and the Staff Manual respectively. Title Pages will be prepared in manuscript.

# WAR DIARY
*or*
~~INTELLIGENCE SUMMARY~~
*(Erase heading not required.)*

(2)

Army Form C. 2118

| Place | Date | Hour | Summary of Events and Information | Remarks and references to Appendices |
|---|---|---|---|---|
| BIENVILLERS | | | | |
| 4.1.17 | | | Lieut F PERKINS returned from leave | |
| 5.1.17 | | | 2/Lieut C.H. ARKWRIGHT returned from leave | |
| 6.1.17 | | | Bombardment of enemy Com Trenches took place by 46th D.A. and VII Corps H.A. | app 54 |
| 7.1.17 | | | Lieut H RYDER proceeded to H.Q. 46th DIV ARTY for attachment. | |
| 8.1.17 | | | 2/Lieut STEVENS joined the Brigade and was posted to B/232 Batty. | |
| 9.1.17 | | | 46th Divisional artillery carried out first part of 46th Divisional artillery OO No 127 bombardment of Enemys tracks dumps and trench railways | app 55 |
| 10.1.17 | | | Group received Two aeroplane calls for Guns firing. Divisional artillery carried out second part of OO No 127. Captain ~~Hayes~~ HAYNES C/232 returned from leave. | |

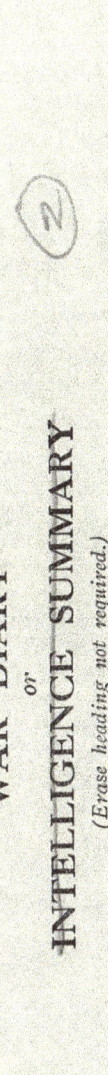

Instructions regarding War Diaries and Intelligence Summaries are contained in F. S. Regs., Part II. and the Staff Manual respectively. Title Pages will be prepared in manuscript.

# WAR DIARY
*or*
# ~~INTELLIGENCE SUMMARY~~
*(Erase heading not required.)*

(3)

Army Form C. 2118

| Place | Date | Hour | Summary of Events and Information | Remarks and references to Appendices |
|---|---|---|---|---|
| BIENVILLERS | | | | |
| 11.1.17 | | | Nothing to report. | |
| 12.1.17 | | | B Batty dispersed large enemy working party compiled at 400 men causing casualties. Enemy shelled D Batty's billets at night causing 4 casualties Dr DEUCHAR killed Sergt WITHERS, Gnrs CULLEN, EVANS, and CLEGG wounded | |
| 13.1.17 | | | Lieuts HICKMAN and CROMBIE proceeded to be medically examined for R.F.C C and D Battys carried out bombardment of enemys trenches in accordance with CRA OO No 130. It was believed that gas cylinders were broken and D/232 continued bombardment during afternoon. Enemy shelled BIENVILLERS hitting D/232 officers mess | app 56 |
| 14.1.17 | | | Lieut R P POCKNEY Joined Brigade for Six days course attached to B/232 Batty Enemy again shelled BIENVILLERS between 8 PM and 10.30 PM. | |
| 15.1.17 | | | Bde and Batty commanders proceeded to report to CRA 14 Division at WARLUS to reconnoitre new positions. D/232 fired successfully on enemy party inflicting Several casualties. Lieut ACKROYD returned from leave. | |

1875 Wt. W593/826 1,000,000 4/15 J.B.C. & A. A.D.S.S./Forms/C. 2118.

Instructions regarding War Diaries and Intelligence Summaries are contained in F. S. Regs., Part II. and the Staff Manual respectively. Title Pages will be prepared in manuscript.

# WAR DIARY
*or*
# ~~INTELLIGENCE SUMMARY~~
*(Erase heading not required.)*

Army Form C. 2118

(4)

| Place | Date | Hour | Summary of Events and Information | Remarks and references to Appendices |
|---|---|---|---|---|
| BIENVILLERS | 16.1.17 | | Lt Drufton returned from leave - quiet day | |
| | 17/1/17 | | Lt Drufton went to Hospital - Lt Ryder returned Div. Arty. H.Q. - Capt Salt went on artillery course in England - Capt Shaw went on leave - | |
| | 18/1/17 | | 2nd Lts Jones and Davenport were attached to this Bde - Lt Joyce went on leave - the 46th Div Arty: bombarded enemy roads and tracks during the night - | App 57 |
| | 19/1/17 | | Nothing to report - except very hard frost set in | |
| | 20/1/17 | | Capt Haynes and Lt Hay went to hospital - 2nd Lt Birch returned from leave - quiet day - 2nd Lt Pockney returned to England - | |
| | 21/1/17 | | Nothing to report - | |
| | 22/1/17 | | Lt Wilson returned from leave - quiet day | |
| | 23/1/17 | | Nothing to report - | App 57 |
| | 24/1/17 | | Enemy Roads and tracks were shelled - otherwise a quiet day - | |

1875 Wt. W593/826 1,000,000 4/15 J.B.C. & A. A.D.S.S./Forms/C. 2118.

Instructions regarding War Diaries and Intelligence Summaries are contained in F. S. Regs., Part II. and the Staff Manual respectively. Title Pages will be prepared in manuscript.

# WAR DIARY
*or*
# INTELLIGENCE SUMMARY
*(Erase heading not required.)*

(5)

Army Form C. 2118

| Place | Date | Hour | Summary of Events and Information | Remarks and references to Appendices |
|---|---|---|---|---|
| BIENVILLERS | 25/1/17 | | Nothing to report | |
| | 26/1/17 | | Lt Brunton went on leave - quiet day - | |
| | 27/1/17 | | Nothing to report | |
| | 28/1/17 | | Lt Col Gisborne went on leave - quiet day - Major Lee returned from leave | |
| | 29/1/17<br>30/1/17 | | Nothing to report | |
| | 31/1/17 | | quiet day, we bombarded Enemy roads & tracks during the night | app 57 |

J Maxwell
Major for
Lt Col.
Cmdg 232 Bde R.F.A.

1875 Wt. W593/826 1,000,000 4/15 J.B.C. & A. A.D.S.S./Forms/C. 2118.

WAR DIARY

or

INTELLIGENCE SUMMARY.

(Erase heading not required.)

| Place | Date | Hour | Summary of Events and Information | Remarks and references to Appendices |
|---|---|---|---|---|
| [illegible]ERS | 1/2/17 | | We bombarded enemy trenches just North of GOMICOURT otherwise quiet day | |
| | | | Nothing to report. | |
| | 3/2/17 | | 2nd Lieut Boden was posted to this Bde and 2nd Lt Parker attached from D.A.C. — This group extended its line B/232 Battery leaving the group and C/231 (6 guns) D/231 (2 guns) came into the group. | |
| | 4/2/17 | | Nothing to report. | |
| | 5/2/17 | | Lieut A. W. Joyce returned from leave | |
| | 6/2/17 | | Lieut Blake went on leave | |
| | 7/2/17 | | Lieut Crombie went on a Signalling Course — Enemy Artillery very Active | |
| | [illegible] | | Lieut Lufton returned from hospital — We bombarded MONCHY. Salient quiet day. | |
| | 9/2/17 | | Lieut Crombie returned from Signalling Course. | |
| | 10/2/17 | | Nothing to report. | |
| | 11/2/17 | | Lieut Crombie proceeded to R.F.C. | |
| | | | Lieut Trevitarick joined the Bde | |
| | | | Enemy shelled dump in St Cross St in the evening. We replied on dump in E12A. | |
| | 12/2/17 | | Bombarded enemy roads and tracks during night 12/13. | |
| | | | Col [illegible] returned from leave | |

Army Form C. 2118.

# WAR DIARY
*or*
# INTELLIGENCE SUMMARY
*(Erase heading not required.)*

Instructions regarding War Diaries and Intelligence Summaries are contained in F. S. Regs., Part II. and the Staff Manual respectively. Title pages will be prepared in manuscript.

| Place | Date | Hour | Summary of Events and Information | Remarks and references to Appendices |
|---|---|---|---|---|
| ENVILLERS | 13/2/17 | | Enemy shelled our supports north of HANNESCAMPS. We replied on his supports South of MONCHY. | |
| | 14/2/17 | | Enemy shelled Battalion H.Q in Shell St. We replied on his Battalion H.Q South of MONCHY. | |
| | | | A/232 provided covering fire for 18 pdr gun & 6" How firing a test | App 62. |
| | 16/2/17 | | Capt Salt returned from Artillery course in England. | |
| | | | Enemy gas-shelled LIVERPOOL St at 9 am and GAS 21 received from 138 Inf Bde, as the wind was unfavourable for a hostile gas attack, the situation was soon determined. | |
| | | | Retaliation for the hostile shelling was carried out at 10 pm. | |
| | 17/2/17 | | Battery Commanders proceeded to BEAUMETZ to reconnoitre positions under 49th Div. Arty. | |
| | 18/2/17 | | Nothing to report | |
| | 19/2/17 | | Lt Hickman bitten by a horse & sent to C.C.S. Lt Pyper leaves Brigade for [illegible] Corps Ammunition Park | |

Army W. W[illegible] Forms/C2118/13.

Instructions regarding War Diaries and Intelligence Summaries are contained in F. S. Regs., Part II. and the Staff Manual respectively. Title pages will be prepared in manuscript.

Army Form C. 2118.

# WAR DIARY
*or*
# INTELLIGENCE SUMMARY.
*(Erase heading not required.)*

| Place | Date | Hour | Summary of Events and Information | Remarks and references to Appendices |
|---|---|---|---|---|
| [illegible]NVILLERS | [illegible]/2/17 | | Nothing to report. | |
| | 21/2/17 | 3-0 am | Inf. Brigade received call Across X. B. C. D. batteries fired for about an hour and a quarter. [illegible] raid, probably prevented by our artillery fire. M.O. returns from hospital. | |
| | 22/2/17 | | Nothing to report. | |
| | 23/2/17 | | Nothing to report. | |
| | 24/2/17 | | 2nd Lt. [illegible] joined the Brigade. | |
| | 25/2/17 | 11-30 pm | Shoot on roads and tracks commenced. | |
| | 26/2/17 | | Shoot on roads and tracks continued until 6. am and repeated later during the day. | |
| | 27/2/17 | | Nothing to report. | |
| | 28/2/17 | | GOMMECOURT occupied by us during the night [illegible] | |

Wt. W. [illegible] 1917. D. D. & L. Ltd. Forms/C.2118/14.

www.ingramcontent.com/pod-product-compliance
Lightning Source LLC
Chambersburg PA
CBHW081356160426
43192CB00013B/2421